TOWARDS A CIVIL ARCHITECTURE IN AMERICA

TOWARDS A CIVIL ARCHITECTURE IN AMERICA

MODULUS 23

THE ARCHITECTURAL REVIEW AT THE UNIVERSITY OF VIRGINIA

MCMXCV

Editor
Adonica Lynnette Inzer

Production Editor
Phillip Glenn Koski

Assistant Production Editor
Michael Gregg

Thematic Editor
M. Lindsay Bierman

Director of Finance
Lee Doar

Assistant Director of Finance
Gillian Goodwin

Director of Distribution
Chris Piwonka

Director of Publicity
Emily Mueller

Faculty Advisor
Robert D. Dripps, 3rd

Associate Editors
Victoria Ballard
Sallah Baloch
Jason Johnson
Andy Kim
Deanna Mabry
Dino Marcantonio
Kamala Mostert
Chris Piwonka
Jennifer Stevenson
Carlos Tan
Roy Wroth

Staff
Amy Beckman
Anne Fletcher
Molly Guenzer
Jennifer Langford
Celia Liu
Alyson Steele
Joshua Chambers
Whitney Morrill
Patrick Byrne

Distributed by Princeton
Architectural Press.
37 East Seventh Street
New York, New York
10003

Cover: Photography by
Christopher Faust.

ISBN   1-56898-037-X
ISSN   0191-4022

CONTENTS

INTRODUCTION

ADONICA LYNNETTE INZER

Modulus 23 investigates how the American cult of individual freedom can by reconciled with a civil ideal in American architecture. While daily life in America rests on the self-assurance of individual rights already won through the efforts of the founding fathers, the ideals of a participatory democracy cannot be guaranteed by the Constitution alone. Having given up the discourse which has sustained democracy since its founding, many Americans have retreated to the isolating environments of an expanding suburban oasis. Contemporary urban planning reduces our civic squares to corporate parks, our public streets to highway arterials, and our public dialogue to prescriptive journalism.

In contrast, America's historic meeting houses, public squares, and city streets stand as monuments to a revolutionary achievement: an unprecedented synthesis of pastoral and civil ideals. *Modulus 23* seeks to discover this synthesis in contemporary America. The embodiment of the civic realm through architecture is essential to the continuation of the American experiment; the physical setting being interdependent with the political activity. Only through a reinvestment in the architecture of the public realm can we further the civic exchange necessary to foster the American project.

The articles and projects collected here explore, compare, and reflect upon the models and ideals which have shaped the historic and the contemporary American civic realm. Through revisiting the founding ideals of American democracy and studying those environments which assisted their growth, the means to instill a fulfilling and rich civil architecture can be discovered; an architecture which honors the political and social life of its citizens. Although answers are elusive, and singular solutions rare, only through an invested critical discourse can we as a nation guard against the increasing peril of civic atrophy.

THE AUTHORITY OF THE CITY LIMIT
AND THE REPRESENTATION OF THE URBAN EDGE

NEAL PAYTON

It is utterly essential for man that he sets his own limits, but of his own free will, that means that he can remove these limits again, or place himself beyond them.

Georg Simmel, *Brucke und Tur* [1]

Neal Payton is Associate Professor of Architecture at Catholic University of America and an architect in Washington, D.C.

Public man and woman represent something of an endangered species.[2] Destruction of their habitat, specifically the civil landscape of the twentieth century, is at least partly to blame. The city, historically the locus of public life, is now more a generalized locale than it is a political entity constituted as a legible representation of the civic realm. The current landscape of the American city reveals more about the assertion of individual property rights than a commitment to sustain community life. This debased urban condition has led to a domestication of the modern American who now lacks the requisite knowledge and skills to survive and flourish in a civil environ.

The demise of the civil landscape is an outgrowth of the crisis of representation confronting contemporary American city founders, designers, and inhabitants.[3] It is a condition caused by competing and redundant simulations of the public realm and is most apparent in the erosion of public space; the latter commodity itself being a measure of civic capacity.[4] One manifestation of this crisis is the lack of a clear consensus on either a precise linguistic or spatial definition of the public realm. The excessive hand wringing by critics of architecture and culture over Disney's themeparks and the Mall(s) of America gives evidence to the fascination of intellectuals over these

Edward Savage, "The Washington Family."

pseudo-public, yet obviously private, realms. Others will admit a bias toward the freeway as the most adequate representation of the public realm. Meanwhile, technology aficionados tout the metaphorical landscapes of microwaves, fiber optic cables, and electronic interfaces as a possible terrain for a newly reconstituted civic realm.[5] However, few would offer such virtual worlds as total replacements for the face-to-face human interaction that occurs in traditional urban environments.

Clearly, neither the mall, the freeway, the Internet, nor any other truncated manifestation of public life can claim any more than limited authority in defining the sphere of civic cooperation and discourse necessary to generate civic interaction. However, these claims have been so artfully asserted that they have inundated the collective consciousness, thereby necessitating a response. As traditional models of civility become outmoded, new culturally relevant alternatives remain elusive.

Historically, the definition and authority of the civic realm was assured by the myths, traditions and conventions that bound the citizens to a place and to each other. Town limits, whether they were physical or legal, served to place a community in a particular landscape and to define the extent to which common law governed.[6] The immediate challenge of attempting to re-place, specifically to re-situate, the community in a manner that recognizes the fundamental and unique characteristic of place, is a daunting task. The traditional locus of the civic realm, the city, is undergoing its own reexamination and redefinition. It is precisely because of such ambiguities that a renewed examination of the city's limits, for example its boundary lines, must become an essential task of urban production.

In the contemporary North American environment, the call for boundaries may seem nostalgic as the authority of any single representation is easily undermined by a competing and commercially viable alternative. One wistfully hopes for a landscape without the sprawl associated with beltways and suburban connector roads; a civilization absent of "edge cities," those misnamed satellite employment centers that surround every American me-

tropolis.[7] Ironically, it is because of the ease in which a term such as *edge city* is accepted into the popular parlance that the need for civil boundaries is all the more apparent. These entities are nothing more than real estate speculations. Contributing nothing to edging or bounding, these entities have no edges themselves and can only dubiously be termed *cities*. The nomenclature bestows upon these investment instruments an unfulfilled promise: the presence of community. In the discussions at citizen forums, it is the lack of community, the absence of a clear sense of a civic realm and of public life, that is cause for activists' concern. Culpability rests, specifically, in the indefinite demarcation of private holdings and public domains. Yet, it is the nature of a boundary to define these two halves of the civic domain and to mediate between them.[8] In this manner, a boundary aids in assuring a physical locus for public life and a limit of civil authority. This demarcation, whether at the individual property line or at the boundary of the city, remains a vital component of civic life.

Speculation regarding the constitution of the city's limit, and hence the limit of civic authority, is hardly a nostalgic exercise, though it does appear a more taxing dilemma than in previous centuries. Now one must ask whether a single hieroglyph or a unitary legend can represent any metropolitan area. No one thing adequately stands for the competing and overlapping constituencies of a city like Los Angeles—a city which one critic has termed the "Rome of post-modern culture."[9] Even Washington, D.C., a city of more defined purpose, supports any number of representations with equal authority. The district's constitutionally mandated ten-mile square, the Beltway, the boundaries of its air-traffic control, the transmitter ranges of its television stations, the areas served by its reservoirs, and the general limits of circulation of *The Washington Post* are all somewhat valid limits of its terrain.

By what means, then, can representation assist in defining, and therefore reconstituting, the civic realm? One must start by examining the activity at its root; to de-*fine* is to make a limit or an edge, and/or to inscribe with meaning. In this context, the act of defining the civic realm is to consider the limits of the city and ultimately to represent it. Baltimoreans and Washingtonians, for example, furiously assert their distinctiveness, yet the experience of the region suggests the contrary.

To limit the city—or *lime* it, to mark it and/or make it concrete—is to bound and ordain the civic realm. Such an immobilizing act may take a variety of forms. Economic concerns, defense requirements or simply an act of poetry or of ritual that acknowledges man's nature as one distinct from that of other creatures, may offer sources for the form.

To bound is to enclose, and to be bound is to be tied or linked to a place or to fellow citizens. The seemingly static form of the boundary, however, conceals the heterogeneity of the *civitas* and the dynamism of its origination under a "homogeneous structure of jurisprudence."[10]

This dynamic and multivalent condition of the civic boundary is worth exploring, as it provides clues to the recovery of public life. It also suggests that an essential focus of architectural production at the end of the twentieth century ought to be the exploration of the representation of the city. This might take the form of a speculation on the nature of the civic realm's definition and limitation, and the authority by which these conditions are determined. What follows is an anthology of bounding stories and histories that might serve as working metaphors for conceptualizing a number of edge phenomena. In turn, these may allow city designers and citizens alike to begin conceptualizing appropriate forms of urban definition, limitation, and representation.

THE PARADIGMATIC CITY LIMIT

How can man withdraw himself from the fields?
Where will he go, since the earth is one huge
unbounded field? Quite simple; he will mark off
a portion of this field by means of walls, which
set up an enclosed finite space over and against

amorphous, limitless space...The urbs *or the* polis *starts by being an empty space, the* forum, *the* agora *and all the rest is just a means of fixing that empty space, of limiting its outlines...*[11]

The presence of a defining element, such as an enclosing wall, does not assure a place-centered or civic realm *a priori*. Its existence does, however, assist in asserting the identity of the community housed inside and differentiates this community from all others. It assists in the representation of a community and in the manifestation of the image by which a community can assert itself. Furthermore, it accomplishes this in a manner reflective of and consistent with the ethical standards of that community.

Medieval London, seen from afar, derived its character from its protective wall. The word *borg* is a term of Northern European origin which carried an original meaning of earthen wall or fort. The term became so closely connected with the image of town that, for medieval Northmen, it came to denote "city."[12]

Ancient Rome was delineated by an enclosure of legendary origin, the significance of which is apparent in the many ways in which this myth was depicted and recorded.[13] According to the legend of the founding of Rome, as reported by Plutarch, citizenship was not without loss of some individual license and required the assumption of personal responsibility for the well-being of the city. As a variation on a Trojan game in which youths on horseback would trace the path of a circle, the founder plowed a deep circumferential furrow around the *mundus*. A circular pit was dug and consecrated as the town center. Along the inside of this furrow, known as a *pomoerium*, a wall was built. At those places where entrance to the city was to be gained, the plow was lifted in order to leave a gap denoting the exception of the gates while still connoting the protection afforded by the wall.[14] The gate signified the place of exchange between inside and out. It formed the transition from the broad open country to the narrow and confined streets of town. By controlling access to the town, the gate had a political function as well. It implied a point at which behavior was to be modified; where rules were to be

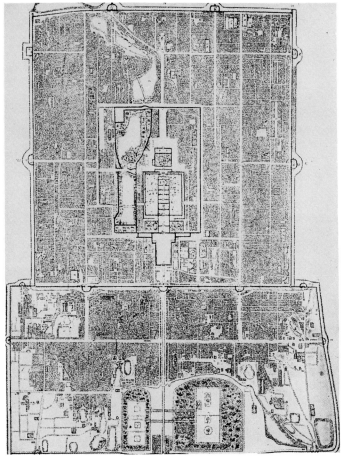

1. Plan of Beijing.

enshrined the founding of Rome, while the inscribed boundary stones secured the site's definition and placated the god Terminus or Jupiter. This combination of artifacts, festivals and inscriptions combined to determine the shape of the city while anchoring the ritual to the ground and the place.[17]

The assertion that the wall may have been a mere defensive measure is not likely, though its erection clearly acknowledges a perceived need to feel secure.[18] The protection afforded by the wall and the myth of its creation would have been as much spiritual or cosmological as it was physical, and indeed for the Romans these two concerns would have seemed inseparable. In a culture where the artifact of the city plays as vital a role in the citizen's well-being as does the house, the making of the ritual urban edge is analogous to the raising of domestic walls. It announces man's vulnerability and distinguishes, architecturally, a particular characteristic of his humanity.[19] The resulting figure on the landscape contains the artifacts of civilization while accommodating the demands of defense, traffic, and commerce.

By the time of republican Rome's demise, the *pomoerium* had lost its significance in controlling the city's boundary. Eventually, the foundation ritual survived only as a significant ceremony to establish the concept of limits. Plowing, as Rykwert suggests, was understood as an act of cosmological significance uniting the earth and sky.[20]

Unlike Rome, the archetypal Chinese city is a square which defines the area within and at the same time gives meaning to the world outside (fig. 1). Its origins are based more on an abstraction of time and space than on a particular ritual. Its shape is also defined by walls. The palace city of Beijing is twice enclosed, first by the bastions of the Forbidden City and second by those of the city proper. Far beyond these walls is the Great Wall of China. Outside of this, the barbarians or outsiders dwell. A long avenue of approach connects the Forbidden City to the world outside, requiring several breaches in the enclosing walls. Historians have pointed to the significance of these breaches as demonstrated by the numerous rituals proliferated at these junctures. Outside the

obeyed.[15] Entering through the gates was, as Rykwert suggests, "an act of covenant with those inside the wall through which the gate leads."[16] So sacred was this pact, so inviolate this enclosure, that the consequence for its transgression was death. Indeed it is reported that Romulus, the legendary founder of Rome, killed his twin brother Remus for taking indiscriminate license and shunning his personal responsibility by daring to jump across the ditch surrounding the wall.

Recurring festivals and monuments commemorated and

Gate of the Noonday Sun, for example, the new candidates for Civil Service would murmur their thanks outside to the gates and walls.

THE NORTH AMERICAN URBAN EDGE

Early American towns and villages, especially those in New England where populations were homogeneous and authority well defined, were delimited by equally conventional if less legendary representations. The relationship of each citizen to another as well as to the community as a whole and the landscape beyond was well defined (fig. 2). It is in this context that one can ask by whose terms the civil landscape can be defined and by what authority its limits can be set.

John Stilgoe has tied the origins of the North American city, particularly the New England village community, to the medieval *landschaft*. The term had more than spatial implications; it was uncritically accepted as the symbol of all order. The entire social, economic, and political structure of the place was encompassed by the term. Typical of the *landschaft* was an intimate relation of fields and clustered structures. The New England village community was characterized by a number of modest dwellings and structures crowded together within a circle of pasture and planting fields and surrounded by unimproved marsh or forest.[21]

The Anglo-Saxons understood the forest as a *wylderness*; the nest or lair of a wild beast. Hence, bewilderment meant confronting the vicissitudes of the wild; the fighting off of wolfpacks, boars and bears. To be bewildered also meant acknowledging a fragmentation of the *landschaft*, a break between man and nature; observing the true fragility of civilized order. Wilderness, in short, identified those spaces beyond human control, the spaces of bewilderment.

At the edge of this arrangement was the march, a border area of some sanctity between grazing fields and the forest. This latter feature was not merely botanical, but was legal or *foris;* land

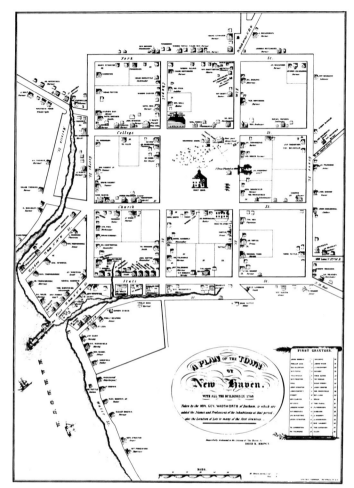

2. Plan of New Haven, 1748.

outside the common law and subject to a special law that safeguarded the king's hunting.[22] The king's hunting forest, in turn, was considered the source of his spiritual connection to God.

Early European settlers in North America transformed this relationship into the distinctive New England village community, seen in the sharp break between village and country.[23] Though the edges of these villages were not defined by discrete walls, but by the absence of any enclosing device, the transition into the wilderness in order to farm or plow the land reinforced the daily

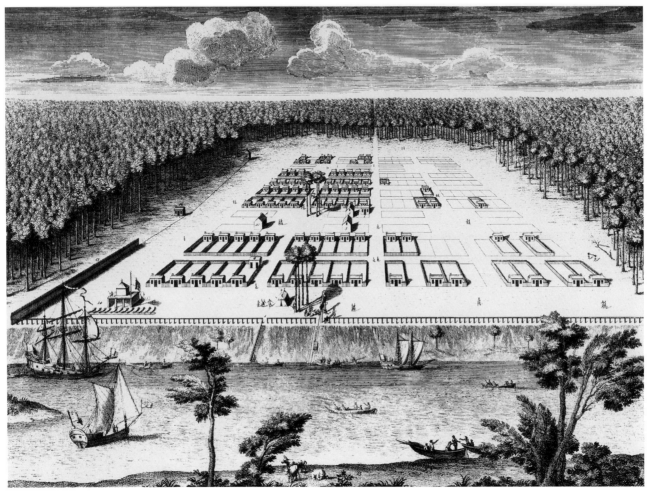

3. Peter Gordon's etching of Savannah, 1734.

ritual of exiting from and returning to the village. The virtual enclosure of the town proper was not authorized by any superior magistrate but rather required community agreement for determination. It is likely that the village edge was maintained for social, political, and religious reasons, as there is little evidence of an attempt at any organized aesthetic experience.

Peter Gordon's famous etching of Savannah portrays this relationship of between village and country (fig. 3). The depiction speaks not of territory stretching to western horizons but of natural limits. It clearly indicates that one of the founder's first tasks was the demarcation of the town's boundary. The limitation of territory in this manner represented a form of contract between town founder and citizen, mutually and freely agreed upon. To further clarify this condition, the limitation was noted in the deed of land that the settler received.[24]

Gordon's rendering also identifies a clear demarcation between the garden zones, those devised by man, and the surrounding wilderness. The edge is created by contradictory acts; those

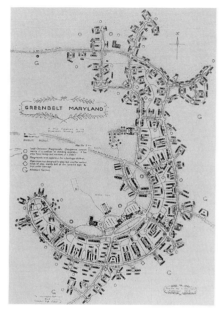

4. Plan of Greenbelt, Maryland.

5. Plan of Greendale, Wisconsin.

of building and carving at the edge of the forest. Both acts evoke the poetic potential of the boundary as the archetypal container of family or cultural rituals. The cultural and social relevance of the natural enclosure is evidenced by the persistence of this pattern of development until the middle of the nineteenth century, with each new ward clearly marked as a separate but interconnected precinct.

Several centuries later, the United States Resettlement Administration under the direction of Rexford Guy Tugwell proposed, once again, to nestle and contain a community within the forest's curative hold. The greenbelt towns Greenbelt, Maryland; Greendale, Wisconsin; Greenbrook, New Jersey; and Greenhills, Ohio proposed by the Roosevelt Administration used topography and a protective edge of forest land to limit growth (figs. 4-7). The intention was to initiate a resettlement program based loosely on the model of Ebenezer Howard's garden cities. The forest was transformed from a spiritual locus with all its transcendent possibilities to both a didactic hieroglyph sugges-

tive of the kind of community housed within, and to a device for growth containment.[25] The latter was a role that, in the twentieth century, had assumed great importance and one for which the forest was well suited.

The greenbelt towns of the Roosevelt administration were more of a final attempt at civic enclosure than representative models of twentieth century urban development. The demise of such bounding standards, however, had began several centuries earlier. These boundaries separated a knowable and ordered world from an unknowable or chaotic one. As early as 1623, Governor Bradford of the Plymouth Colony was lamenting the disintegration of the compact spatial unit of the town.

> For now as their stocks increased...there was no longer any holding them together...And no man now thought he could live, except he had catle and a great deale of ground to keep them; all striving to increase their stocks by which means they were scatered all over the bay, quickly, and

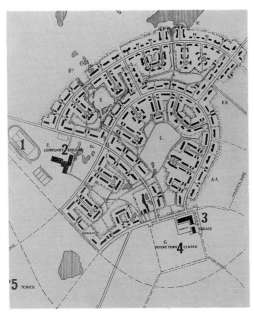

6. Plan of Greenbrook, New Jersey.

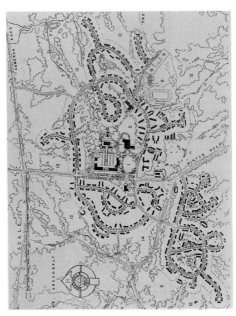

7. Plan of Greenhills, Ohio.

the town, in which they lived compactly till now, was left very thine, and in a short time allmost desolate...And this, I fear, will be the ruine of New-England, at least of the Churches of God ther.[26]

At the time, Governor Bradford's concerns may have seemed unwarranted. Hundreds of North American towns developed throughout the eighteenth, nineteenth, and early twentieth centuries as compact spatial units. As late as 1957, Colin Rowe and John Hejduk were able to describe such western villages as Leadville, Colorado; Carson City, Nevada; and Globe, Arizona as "potent symbols of urbanity by reason of the emptiness, through which they are approached."[27] The remoteness of these locales alone cannot fully explain the persistence of these patterns, as even now in such Maryland towns as New Market and Burkitsville, spatial control is exerted by a lacunar edge whose significance is, at the least, political in nature (fig. 8).

Nonetheless, the vast majority of North American develop-

ments fell prey to the centrifugal forces feared by Governor Bradford. The rise of the railroad and, even more significantly, the automobile only exacerbated the condition. Planners attempted to rationalize the city by promoting the most efficient land organization, substituting functional zoning for spatial control. Village edges and even town and city boundaries were easily transgressed, dislocating the harmonious natural order that existed in early American communities.[28] As the city's geography became increasingly specialized and fragmented, distances between differing land uses increased exponentially. Small, contained, identifiable communities became difficult to sustain if not outright illegal. In large cities, neighborhoods which historically had been microcosms of the city itself tilted towards homogeneity in use. Civic space, conventionally the most critical constituent of any neighborhood, was so degraded by this change in land use that it ceased being a significant component of metropolitan areas.

Admittedly, some boundaries were more difficult to trans-

8. View of Burkitsville, Maryland.

gress. In particular, many were imposed by the landscape directly, internalized socially and accepted as a virtual artifice, a man-made vessel containing the ritual and mythical potential of earlier examples. Boston owes its pre-twentieth century form to such an edge. Though it developed without a plan, at least until the late nineteenth century, its growth was controlled by convention, and by the edge imposed by geography. Bostonians have been known to describe their city as a state of mind surrounded by water.[29] New York and San Francisco are similarly defined.

In 1918, with the growth of the North American metropolis already out of control, Charles Mulford Robinson wrote of the sea as the best place from which to view the contemporary city. The water, in his eyes, provided the neutral foreground out of which the city center appears as a collective whole. It was the threshold that traditional cities had always possessed but which was no longer extant on land entries to or exits from the city.[30] Pittsburgh, the three rivers city, has a virtual palisade to its south such that access to the city is controlled and channeled through tunnels

burrowed through the mountainside. The approach offers a spectacular drama, leading such diverse critics as Paul Goldberger and Prince Charles to declare it the most beautiful of any entrance to an American city (fig. 9).

The significance of such a threshold is nowhere more apparent than in the memory of the funeral march for a slain president. The image of a hearse and a procession leaving Washington, traversing Memorial Bridge and the river it spans, and, finally, passing the gates marking the entrance of Arlington National Cemetery, is one of the premier examples of the edge, the threshold, and the gate operating together in the service of civic life. The nation watched as John F. Kennedy departed the city from which he governed. The existence of this route owes as much to circumstance as it does to design, but this does not diminish the achievement or the recognition of its potential.[31] The city defined and its gate thus represented raised the funeral of a president to the level of spectacle worthy of the anguish and remorse of the populace. The catharsis of a collective mourning

9. Highway entry into Pittsburgh from the south.

was achieved.

The boundary of L'Enfant's plan for a nation's capital was defined equally by the threshold of the river as by its topography. Along the city's confines to the north and northeast rise escarpments, to its west lays Rock Creek, and to its east, the Anacostia River. Even today one can see tremendous changes in density in the patterns of development north of what was known as Boundary Road. This street, now called Florida Avenue, is a winding lane that traces the original edge (fig. 11). Atop the escarpments are situated a series of campuses supporting public works and institutions. These facilities include a reservoir, two public schools with their adjoining playing fields, and a city park. Each of these vantage points has traditionally provided views of the Capitol and what is known as the monumental core.[32] Their location at the edge suggests an intentional effort at limiting the growth of the city and providing for an almost arcadian landscape beyond it, from which the broad expanse of the city might be defined and represented.

THE RECONFIGURED CITY LIMIT

Contemporary efforts at representing urban definition have had perhaps no more heroic a practitioner than the Frenchman Tony Garnier in his early twentieth century proposal for the *Cite Industrielle*, though Garnier's written description of the proposal, with its modernist sympathies, seems to discount the significance of any defining edges: "the land of the town as a whole is like a large park, with no enclosing wall to limit the grounds."[33] The illustrations, however, reveal another agenda. The south edge of town is established by an embankment lined with civic buildings and a park-like promenade overlooking a valley.

The mountainous northern edge of Garnier's city is reinforced by the artifice of an enormous hydroelectric dam (fig. 12). Festooned with water pipes and a giant stairway, this monumental construction celebrates the generation and incorporation of electric power into the city. In this view of the town's proposed metallurgical factory, the significance of this edge is apparent

10. Plan of Washington, D.C.

both as a vessel and also as the source of power for the factory (fig. 13). Atop the dam, a tree-lined motorway is equipped with viewing ledges. The traveler is allowed a panoramic vista when entering the city from the north, which reveals at once the dependency of the city upon the edge for its very existence. The dam as edge is celebrated as the defining component of the city itself.

While the site for Garnier's fabrication was purely hypothetical, the 9-1/2 square mile level plain designed by L'Enfant to seat the federal government of the newly constituted United States was quite specific.[34] Adjacent to and including many of George Washington's land holdings, the site straddled the Potomac River. The first president thought this navigational highway would promote the development of the west and, ultimately, the American empire.[35] Washington's vision is articulated in Edward Savage's depiction of "The Washington Family" (Frontispiece). In this view, a seated Washington rests one arm atop the plan of the city, seen spread upon the table at which Martha also

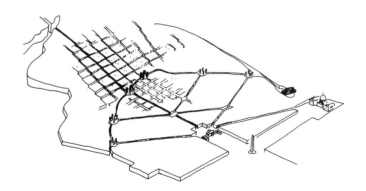

11. Diagram of Florida Avenue.

12. Tony Garnier, Aerial view of Water Dam.

sits. Behind the pair is a view west, up the Potomac to the vast hinterlands of the North American continent. Washington's right arm sits upon the shoulder of Martha's grandson, George Washington Parke Custis. The boy, signifying the future of the nation, in turn, lays his hand upon a globe.

Savage's allegorical painting is suggestive of the paradox of American urbanism.[36] The map itself, with its clearly articulated bounded terrain, suggests the limit to which civil authority extends. Juxtaposed against both the view of a boundless landscape and the tantalizing presence of the world, in the guise of the globe, all of the ingredients of the dilemma are in place. The limits of the city, whether a product of geography, artifice, ritual, or defense, provide a protective and civilizing envelope. But the boundaries denied promise great wealth and power.

Within the mythology of North America, obstacles in the landscape are often thought of not as limits, but as opportunities. The move west, for example, is a tale of frontiers crossed and boundaries violated. In St. Louis a great parabolic arch was built to commemorate such transgressions. The Jefferson National Expansion Memorial, the arch, is a gateway at the edge of the Mississippi River. Its enormous size and its position within the city clearly indicate its significance as a monument to the purchase of the Louisiana Territory and the opening of the West. In just twenty-five years this monument has been co-opted as the symbol of the city in which it stands. The irony exists in the erasure of over thirty-five square blocks of sturdy brick buildings which originally stood on the grassy field. This act is all the more profound because these same thirty-five blocks roughly represent the original area of the walled city of St. Louis (figs. 14-16).

Even as a modicum of life returns to downtown St. Louis and the waterfront, city fathers have signaled that this arch does not allow entrance to the city. At a recent Independence Day celebration, the gate was as usual, transparent. However, the pedestrian bridges crossing the Mississippi River from East St. Louis were closed, limiting entry to St. Louis only to those who owned cars. The urban poor of East St. Louis, whose deteriorated

13. Tony Garnier, Metallurgical Factory.
View of furnaces.

housing would look across to the great parabola Saarinen de-signed if it weren't for the interstate highway in between, had, paradoxically, a more difficult time participating in the celebra-tion of freedom than their proximity should warrant. The tragedy is in the emptiness of the mythic significance of this monument—its reduction to sign alone. There may be a gateway, but there is no act of covenant associated with its through passage.

The political cynicism of this condition is made all the more ironic in light of Walter Seitter's observations that the operator of an automobile is "someone who has procured for himself his own gate, who straps himself into it and then—with the gate surround-ing him—lets himself be driven by it."[37] Such a condition referred to by Richard Sennett as a *purified identity* relates a peculiar ability that modern man and woman have developed to separate themselves from the rest of the world, and to distance themselves by a rigid self-definition.[38] With no other forms of protection from a still hostile and indefinite world, domestic walls, in whatever their form, are the only means at modern man's and woman's disposal.

Contemporary boundaries are not intended to protect us from the disorder of an unknowable world, but rather from the rabble of an undesirable ethnic, socioeconomic, or political group next door. Such boundaries are rarely mutually self-imposed. As in the walls of the Warsaw Ghetto, or the Berlin wall, they imprison as much as they protect.[39] Though they are, more often than not, physically innocuous, intangible abstrac-tions, their effects can be monumental, and experienced as viscerally as the Berlin wall. The implications of the red lines on an insurance company's map, the color-coded districts on a planner's land use plan, or the dotted lines around a legally defined historic district, walling out change and its unknown consequences, are all well known.

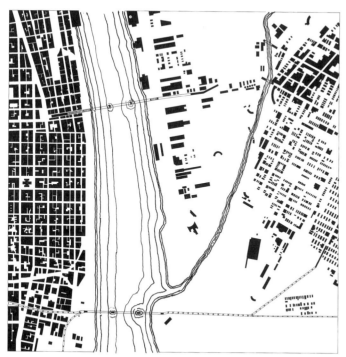

14. Plan of St. Louis, c. 1910.

15. Plan of St. Louis, c. 1988.

TOWARDS A REPRESENTATION OF THE URBAN EDGE

The North American metropolis of the late twentieth century recalls conditions of the medieval Anglo-Saxon *landschaft*. Once again, bewildering spaces lie outside the civilized order. These suburban spaces seem beyond human control, even though they have been thoroughly planned. This chaos arguably results from a state of being in which the absence of boundaries is more apparent than their presence. For example, large tracts of metropolitan real estate are written off as socially and environmentally dysfunctional, while new stretches of less spoiled terrain are quickly consumed.

In this condition, it is not surprising that modern man and woman have sought the safety and isolation of a *purified identity*. Remedial prescriptions are not easily determined. The utility of historical boundary forms in alleviating such a modern predica-

ment is highly doubtful. The wall, as a constituent element in the modeling of a utopian city, was drawn from the disciplinary order of plague stricken, seventeenth century towns, and therefore has little relevance.[40] More fundamentally, little demand exists for this element of protection from a hostile or literally unknowable world. The artifice of boundary does serve other needs. It is instrumental in distinguishing public man from private; citizen from visitor; even spatial order from disorder.

There is no universal model that would serve to alleviate this condition. Unlike its Roman antecedents, the political edge as it exists in North America is a transparent container of sorts; for example, the boundary that identifies and distinguishes one community, one body politic, from all others. This political edge is independent in shape, in character, and often in size of the population housed within its borders, as most citizens belong to a number of communities simultaneously, a hierarchy of boundaries commingled; villages, townships, parishes, school districts, community associations, special tax districts, union locals, private clubs, etc., each perforated by the other. The resulting web of relationships accords the metropolitan individual a freedom unknown to the small town dweller. Simmel argues that, "the smaller the circle that forms our milieu and the more restricted those relations to others are which dissolve the boundaries of the individual, the more anxiously the circle guards the achievements, the conduct of life, and the outlook of the individual...."[41] According to this reasoning, the free man is the one who stands under the law of the largest social order, rather than under the narrow restrictions of the small town. However, when the overlapping community limits become so ephemeral as to carry no more or less significance than the boundaries of an area code, then modern man's concern need not be for the cosmopolitan freedom for which Simmel has argued but for the permanent political structures that give definition and meaning to civilized life.

The American courthouse square operates in an exemplary manner as a permanent political structure. The principle of authority is embodied in its arrangement and architecturally bounded by a clearly defined public square. The courthouse square dominates the image of the landscape for miles. Rowe and Hejduk noticed this characteristic of the Texas courthouse town when they stated, "If it is not the sight of a water tower, the first indication of arrival at one of them is apt to be the courthouse which appears from a distance of several miles, as the slightest eruption upon the horizon." [42]

The courthouse square operates in a manner similar to that of the Roman forum or the Greek agora. As described by Ortega y Gassett, "The square, thanks to the walls which enclose it, is a portion of the countryside which turns its back on the rest....This lesser rebellious field which secedes from the limitless one, and keeps to itself, is a space *sui generis* of the most novel kind in which man frees himself from the community of the plant and the animal...and creates an enclosure apart which is purely human, a

16. The St. Louis Arch.

civil space."[43] Compelling as it is, the courthouse square as paradigm is limited in its application. Other means and models are of civic identity are also necessary.

Civic life demands that neighborhoods and towns be limited in size and characterized by a heterogeneous mix of activities. In undeveloped areas this means prescribing a limit to a town's growth and endowing it with defining elements, perhaps as simple as greenbelts, stream valleys, or boulevards. In existing areas, it means ascertaining natural and perceptual boundaries so as to strengthen the representation of the existing community. Neighborhoods within cities can and should abut one another, mimicking the pattern that has characterized the growth of London, for example. Linkages between them should be frequent, two-way, and of monumental significance in order to facilitate interconnection and prevent xenophobia.

These small admonishments by no means suggest a longing

17. View of Beltway.

for the metaphoric recovery of the ritual of protection suggested by the legend of Romulus and Remus. The re-creation of long dead rituals is hardly an appropriate means to re-present the city's delineation. The Trojan game these brothers reenacted was a civil act as well as a sacred one. The monumental effect was the establishment of a boundary, an artifact of such significance that it defined and represented the *civitas* of Rome. Regardless of its form—it may be a feature of the landscape, a boulevard, or a series of civic buildings—the city's limit, or the neighborhood's edge, represents the possibility of a civic structure.[44] Its effect is equally monumental, allowing the process of redefining the civilized order to occur.

This is not an argument that begs for a remaking of traditional walls or other specific models from pre-industrial cities.[45] Neither does it accept the frame of the windshield as the only possible gateway left to the modern metropolis. Rather, this essay suggests that the city's limit, no less than its center, possesses a cultural persistence. This demand must be acknowledged if the recovery

of a civic realm, the habitat of public man, is to occur. Such limits are necessary even if, as Simmel suggests, they are ultimately transgressed.

EXCURSUS: THE EDGE OF WASHINGTON

In an effort to find alternatives to the self-detachment of modern life referred to above, an attempt to metaphorically recover one of the city's defining elements is proposed. The Capital Beltway in Washington, D.C., so clearly understood in the popular press as the edge of Washington, seemed an appropriate place upon which to operate. One local politician referred to it as the unifier and definer of the region. In the less than 25 years since its completion, this 190-million dollar public works project has become one of the premier symbols of the nation's capital and of the business of government. "Beltway bandits" (i.e., consultants) roam the

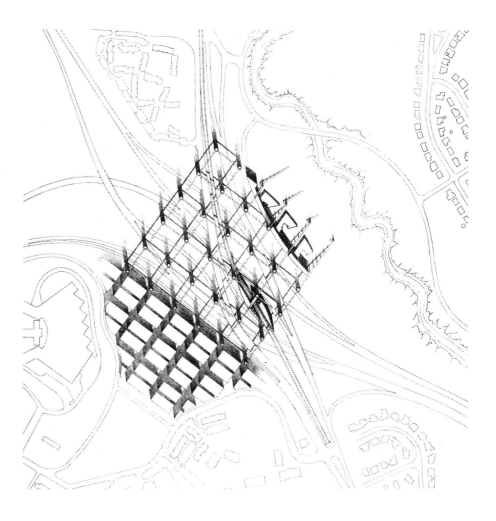

18. Proposed plan at Exits 34 and 35.

edge of this wall ready to pounce on any unsuspecting carrier of federal funds to the hinterlands. Living inside the beltway has taken on ominous implications.[46]

For area residents the Beltway is an often cursed evocation of the region's ever sprawling and congested reach. Carrying upwards of 227,000 vehicles a day, about 40% above its theoretical capacity, its load is expected to hit 300,000 vehicles by the year 2010. A number of major modifications are contemplated by traffic planners, such as widening it to 14 lanes, designating car pool lanes where none exist, installing driver information systems and building a by-pass. These changes are all aimed at allowing still more vehicular traffic. Not surprisingly, none of these proposals envisions any greater civic or symbolic potential of this urban artifact.

The following proposal suggests that the Beltway be treated as a great urban monument (fig. 17). In a sort of reversal of 19th century traditions in which bulwarks around the great European cities were removed and boulevards provided in their place, the scheme envisions a ritual wall metaphorically rising out of the path of the highway.[47] At the interchanges, the places of exchange between inside and out, it is envisioned that projects of a public nature will be constructed. Each of these points are

19. Aerial view of proposal.

acknowledged as gateways, as places where behavior is to modified, and rules obeyed.[48]

The point where I-270 (which becomes I-70 and spans the nation terminating in San Francisco), MD-350 (Rockville Pike, the original turnpike connecting the port of Georgetown with the hinterlands), and the Red Line of the Metrorail subway system converge has been singled out for study (fig. 18). It is an interchange whose sinuous breakdown lanes and off-ramps are simultaneously disorienting and beautiful. The vast space is unoccupiable, except transiently as an occupant of a motorized vehicle. Yet strangely, when seen from above, the view is quite compelling.

The program for this space, along the city's edge at the highways leading out of town, is a prison devoted to corrupt politicians and government officials. Exiled to a sort of urban purgatory, violators of the public trust are neither in the loop nor

are they allowed to escape its daily grind (figs. 19, 20). Upon each point of the grid stands a tower, and in one case a negative tower. Each tower is devoted to a particular crime and houses a representative guilty party. Thus, in parody of Ledoux's houses at Chaux, one sees a house for a moralizing hypocrite, a house for a misogynist, a house for a cover-up co-conspirator, a house for an eavesdropper, a house for a bribe taker, a house for a power abuser, and so on. Like medieval rogues and thieves hung in cages along the highways leading out of town, these abusers of the public trust are held up for ridicule by passing travelers at the edge of the city.

Along the northern boundary of the highway another public institution is envisioned: The College of Democracy. As envisioned by its proposed founders, "It is an educational institution within which individuals may pursue the study of democratic institutions in preparing themselves for future careers as legisla-

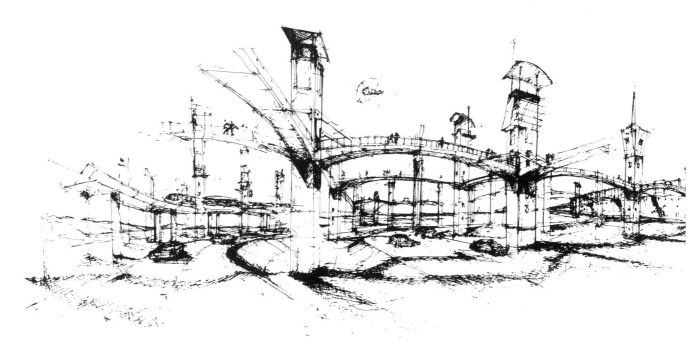

20. View of proposal from highway.

tors and elected representatives."[49] The long wall-like building, proposed to house this noble undertaking, both encloses the space of the interchange and separates it from Rock Creek Park just to the north. As the budding politicians and political operatives stroll the fourth floor stoa of this wall they can overlook either the park or the prison; virtue or corruption. From this vantage point they can contemplate the kind of leaders they aspire to be.

Linking the towers to each other and to the college is a network of pedestrian bridges, suspended an average of 40 feet above the highways. In addition to affording a fantastic view of this marvel of public infrastructure and of the intense use to which it has been put, these bridges allow access to exhibits housed within each tower. The exhibits will tell the story of the crime and the criminal. Members of the public may wish to visit some or all of these exhibits in any order they choose. They may also wish simply to sit upon the bridges, to engage in discourse, or to ponder

and reflect upon the scene. These bridges will also connect the towers and college to the newly created Metro stop, whose 1%-for-art budget will be spent on a monument to the whistle-blower. The bridges further serve to connect a fragment of the city lying to the south of the interchange with the development to the north. Residents living just inside the beltway, previously cut off by the highway interchange from the park and the existing Grosvenor Metro stop, will now have easy access to public transportation as well as to Rock Creek Park. Thus the city, the highway, the prison, and the park are linked, and the gate as "an act of covenant with those inside the wall through which the gate leads"[50] is affirmed.

NOTES

1 Georg Simmel, *Bruck und Tur*.

2 Two of the first to sound the alarm were Hannah Arendt, *The Human Condition* (Chicago: 1958) and Richard Sennett, *The Fall of Public Man* (New York: 1977).

3 The origin of this crisis is, in itself, tangential to the scope of this article. However, in light of the argument by Jean Baudrillard ("The Precession of Simulacra," *Simulations* (New York: 1983)) one is tempted to ask by what criteria—other than the most technical—urban design can be accomplished, when experience is disengaged from setting and the representational characteristic of architecture as an intersubjective interpretation of reality is rarely acknowledged. This is the question posed, in a manner of speaking, by Alberto Perez Gomez in *Architecture and the Crisis of Modern Science* (Cambridge, Mass: MIT Press), 6. Perez-Gomez is referring, in this context, to all of the arts—arguing for their role as a "profound form of knowledge."

4 The concept of *civic capacity* as a form of social capital is discussed in Robert Nelly Bellah, *Habits of the Heart: Individualism and Commitment in American Life* (Berkeley: 1985). In this argument, *civic capacity* is defined as a measure of the willingness and ability of a populace to utilize the shared resource of cooperation to effect the common good, for example to achieve clean air, safe streets, etc. Bellah argues that public space is an essential ingredient in developing the civic habits and networks of trust necessary to build that civic capacity.

5 See, for example, Michael Benedikt, ed., *Cyberspace* (Cambridge, Mass: 1991) and Howard Rheingold, *The Virtual Community: Homesteading on the Electronic Frontier* (Reading, Mass: 1993).

6 For example, Carroll William Westfall credits the Roman Empire's contribution to urbanism as the unification of civil form (*civitas*) with its urban setting (*urbs*). See C.W. Westfall, "Cities," in

C.W. Westfall and Robert Jan Van Pelt, *Architectural Principles in the Age of Historicism* (New Haven: 1991), 281.

7 Joel Garreau, *Edge City* (New York: 1992). This is the term Garreau has coined for such places as Tysons Corner, Virginia and King of Prussia, PA.

8 Aristotle, *The Politics*, Book I, ii.

9 Mike Davis, *City of Quartz: Excavating the Future of Los Angeles* (New York: 1991), 67. He goes on to describe it as a place "in which the city is at once an endless text always promising meaning but ultimately only offering hints and *signs* of a possible and final reality...like a 'printed circuit'—or a freeway."

10 Jose Ortega y Gasset, *The Revolt of the Masses*, translation unknown (New York: 1932), 166-167. He also points out that "a juridical homogeneousness...does not necessarily imply centralization."

11 Ortega y Gasset, *The Revolt of the Masses*, 165-166.

12 Steen Eiler Rasmussen, *London, the Unique City* (Cambridge, Mass: 1982), 31.

13 For example, it is depicted on Roman coins as is the ancient hieroglyph depicting the circle surrounding two cross hairs, the *quadrattura*. See Joseph Rykwert, *The Idea of a Town* (Cambridge, Mass:1988), 67. Examples of other cities commemorating their defining origins include Beirut, Celsa (Spain) and Caesarea. This book is one of a number of sources that describes the ritual surrounding the founding of Rome.

14 Plutarch, *Life of Romulus*, ed. John Dryden, revised by A. H. Clough (London: 1927-28).

15 For a historical account of the political dimension of the gate and the wall see Walter Seitter, "Dismantlement: On the Obscenity of Towns," *Daidalos 13* (West Berlin: 1984).

16 Rykwert, *The Idea of a Town*, 135.

17 Rykwert, *The Idea of a Town*. For Rykwert's assertion of the commemorative and anchoring function of festivals see p. 27. For a discussion of boundary

markers, see pp. 106-117.

18 Rykwert, *The Idea of a Town*, 136. It has been suggested that, in Roman towns there may have even been two walls independent of each other or, alternatively, that towns founded by the Trojan game "and provided with the ritual wall may have had fragmentary defense walls or no defense walls at all."

19 See Arthur Danto, "Abide/Abode" in *Housing: Symbol, Structure, Site*, ed. Lisa Taylor (New York: 1991). Man's humanity is characterized, in this argument, by his distinction from God, that is by an "essential weakness, as beings in need of shelter from the wild world without."

20 Rykwert, *The Idea of a Town*,132. The plow was a symbol and an instrument of fertilization. The Greek word *aurora* meant both "plowed land" and "childbearing woman." Rykwert also reports that classical writers speculating on the etymology of the word *urb*, a city, suggest its derivation from *urvum*, the curve of a plowshare or from *urvo*, for "I plow round," (p. 134).

21 John Stilgoe, *Common Landscapes of America* (New Haven: 1982).

22 J. B. Jackson, "A Pair of Ideal Landscapes," *Reading the Vernacular Landscape* (New Haven: 1984).

23 John Reps, *The Making of Urban America* (Princeton: 1965), 125.

24 The deed read, "Whereas...James Oglethorpe hath set out and limited...a town called Savannah with Lotts for Houses..." Reps, *The Making of Urban America*,187.

25 See Clarence Stein, *Towards New Towns for America* (New York: 1957). Greenbelt was to be "of a size that makes possible a full measure of social life, but no larger," (p. 136). Stein quotes from the "accepted definition of the Garden City." Moreover, he quotes from the "'Report of the Senate Subcommittee,' written by Senator Paul H. Douglas...The particular portion of the amendment relating to adequate open land is intended to preserve as far as practicable the original design of having each of these projects protected by a

green belt of park and forest land surrounding such a community," (p.133).

26 Reps, *The Making of Urban America*, 119.

27 Colin Rowe and John Hejduk, "Lockhart, Texas," *Architectural Record* (March, 1957), 202. A 1990 visit to Globe, Arizona, however, suggests it can no longer be counted in this camp.

28 It should be acknowledged that such a relationship has been referred to as a mythic one, resulting from a nostalgic attempt to overcome the deteriorated conditions of urban life in the 19th century. See Christine Boyer, *Dreaming the Rational City* (Cambridge, Mass: 1983), 3, 31-42. Assuming that the arrangement has been romanticized, it nonetheless allowed for spatially coherent urban environments.

29 Melville C. Branch, *Comparative Urban Design—Rare Engravings:1830-1843* (New York: 1978), 98.

30 Charles Mulford Robinson, *Modern Civic Art or the City Made Beautiful*. (New York: 1918), 41.

31 For a thorough discussion of Arlington Cemetery and its relationship to Washington see Jill Bretherick, "Honor of Sacrifice: the Evolution of Arlington National Cemetery", *Modulus 17* (Charlottesville: University of Virginia School of Architecture, 1984).

32 The campuses, so called because they are public greens at the edge of the city, are Meridian Hill Park, the Banneker School/Recreation Center, the Cardozo High School and its grounds, and the MacMillan Reservoir. A few of these views have been obscured in recent years by new construction. See Committee of 100 of the Federal City, "Recommendations: 14th and U Street Areas" (1989).

33 Tony Garnier, trans. Marguerite E. McGoldrick, *Un Cite Industrielle* (New York: 1989), 14.

34 Kenneth Bowling, *Creating the Federal City, 1774-1800: Potomac Fever* (Washington, DC: 1988), 39-41. For a discussion of Washington's behind the scene's role in site selection see pp. 72-76.

35 Though the mercantile status of the Potomac for which Washington hoped was never achieved, it has been established that the river's significance is nonetheless profound.

36 I am grateful to Patrick Pinnell who brought this painting and its implications for American urbanism to my attention.

37 Seitter, "Dismantlement," 50.

38 Richard Sennett, *The Uses of Disorder* (New York: 1970).

39 While there are many accounts of life within such enclosures, one compelling example can be found in Peter Schneider, *The Wall Jumper* (New York: 1983). With respect to the now destroyed Berlin wall he writes, "The border between the two German states, and especially between the two halves of Berlin, is considered the world's most closely guarded and the most difficult to cross...Two hundred and sixty watchtowers stand along the border ring, manned day and night by twice that many border guards. The towers are linked by a tarred military road, which runs within the border strip. To the right and the left of the road, a carefully raked stretch of sand conceals trip wires; flares go off if anything touches them.. Should this happen, jeeps stand ready for the border troops, and dogs are stationed at 267 dog runs along the way. Access to the strip from the east is further prevented by an inner wall which runs parallel to the outer Wall at an irregular distance. Nail-studded boards randomly scattered at the foot of the inner wall can literally nail a jumper to ground, spiking him on the five-inch prongs. It is true that long stretches of the inner wall still consist of the facades of houses situated along the border, but their doors and windows have been bricked up. Underground in the sewers, the border is secured by electrified fences, which grant free passage only to the excretions of both parts of the city." 52-53.

40 Michel Foucault, *Discipline and Punish; The Birth of the Prison,* trans. Alan Sheridan (New York: 1977), 197-198.

41 Georg Simmel, "The Metropolis and Mental Life," Classic *Essays on the Culture of Cities*, ed. Richard Sennett (New York: 1969), 54.

42 Rowe and Hejduk, "Lockhart, Texas."

43 Ortega y Gasset, *The Revolt of the Masses,* 165.

44 "Structure" is used here in its most general sense, to mean more than building only.

45 History provides us with such an ill-conceived attempt at re-walling a city in the last days of the *ancien regime* in Paris. Despite Ledoux's quixotic and delightful designs for breaches in this wall, the *barrier*, such architectural confections were hardly compensation for what was obviously a taxation ploy of the most regressive nature. Many Parisians lost their heads over the scam and in the ensuing mayhem.

46 Former President Reagan understood this when commenting on the media's continued interest in the Iran-Contra affair. He suggested that those Americans living outside the beltway had lost interest in the story and returned to watching their favorite TV shows. This wall seems to have trapped legislators, lobbyists, and a host of semi-automatic gun-slinging outlaws together in a protective cocoon, fighting amongst themselves but immune from what the former president's advisors must have thought were the catatonic masses.

47 In fact, such walls have already been provided, in the form of precast concrete sound barriers erected around the perimeter.

48 Seitter, "Dismantlement."

49 Mission of the College of Democracy as suggested in the brief supplied by the National Graduate University of Arlington, VA, sponsor of the College of Democracy. The institution's board of directors has no knowledge of this particular proposal and

FIGURE CREDITS

Frontis Courtesy The National Gallery of Art, Andrew W. Mellon Collection, Washington, D.C.

1 Courtesy Yale University Art Library, New Haven.

2 Courtesy New Haven Colony Historical Society.

3 Courtesy Hargrett Library, University of Georgia.

4-7 Courtesy MIT Press.

8 Photo by Author.

9 Courtesy of Greater Pittsburgh Convention and Visitor's Bureau

10, 11 Urban Design Studio, Catholic University, Chinh Doan.

12, 13 Courtesy of Princeton Architectural Press.

14, 15 Urban Design Studio, Washington University, St. Louis.

16 Photo by Author.

All other illustrations courtesy of the author.

ACKNOWLEDGMENTS

Research on this article was supported in part by a grant from the Alfred Kaskell Fund of Syracuse University, School of Architecture. Many thanks go to Ghassan Abukurah, Chinh Doan and Mike Gala for their efforts on the "Edge of Washington" project.

CIVILIANS/CIVIL ALIENS

AN INTERVIEW WITH PETER WALDMAN
BY PHILLIP GLENN KOSKI

WITH EXCERPTS FROM THE BLACKSBURG PROJECT
BY PETER WALDMAN WITH
FARMER PUCKETT WARNER ARCHITECTS

Peter Waldman is a practicing
architect and Chair of the
Department of Architecture at the
University of Virginia.

Modulus interviewed Mr. Waldman in April of 1994, soon after his return from Italy where he served as the director of the University of Virginia's study abroad program in Venice. The following discussion of the 'Blacksburg Project' refers to his entry in the competition, "A Center for Civic Activity in the Town of Blacksburg," held in December of 1992.

Before we discuss the Blacksburg Project I would like to begin by asking about your recent stay in Venice and the studio you conducted there. In particular, I'm interested in your impressions of Venice having lived as a resident of that city—if only for a few months.

We arrived on the 17th of January to a very empty city. That became quite important because a month later was Carnival time and the city filled up with great masses of people. It changed from a desolate city—where one would look at the architecture, the monuments and all that—into an incredibly packed city. We were overwhelmed by the presence of so many people, and in particular the presence of people wearing costumes. There seemed to be an entire population in costume. This became significant because there is this issue in Venice of the city as theater—of deliberate theater, intentional theater, two-dimensional theater in certain ways.

On the very first day, Clemente di Thiene, the professor connected with the program in Venice, took us around to the edge of the Grand Canal near the Ducal Palace, and he showed

"First Indians Ever in Venice"

Scuola San Marco. "Scenario Publico."

us the Palladian churches across the way. He said that at the very moment the Venetian Republic knew it was dying—its economic base drained by competition with the Atlantic trade—the city hired certain architects, Palladio the most famous of them all, to do a number of stage sets so that the city would be remembered for its glory.

By "stage sets" you mean...?

Stage sets meaning façades for existing churches—S. Giorgio Maggiore, Il Redentore, S. Maria dei Miracoli, and so on. In some ways we saw Venice at the best time to photograph it's architecture...that is, when its empty. But after a week we saw that in addition to these permanent stage sets there were these temporary stage sets put up in the piazzas. They had pantomime, music, juggling—things like that. Now, I should say that while we were there the Italian elections were coming up and we got some very real theater as well. There were hundreds of members of the labor unions coming out to the city, filling the square, holding debates, walking around and returning to the transit station. They do use the spaces. They use them, I would say, in a congested way that becomes very much alive.

I would like to bring up this other issue regarding Venice and its situation, historically, as a trading city...of having imported, among other things, many different architectural styles, Byzantine, and Gothic and so on, to make a fundamentally new kind of architecture. The city is an amalgamation of these diverse and foreign influences. And it is successful, perhaps, because it not only tolerated these influences, but celebrated them.

Well, that might be the most important point, which is that unlike Florence and many of the other cities we've visited, Venice is constructed many ways. There is something the Venetians call *sacca*, which is booty taken from many other places. The English call it "nicking", which means picking up or taking pieces of a building. The Venetians raided Constantinople twice, the first time taking incredible relics of the Roman Empire. But then they went back and also sacked the Byzantine relics. They wanted very badly to be associated with a long term power presence, because as a people they were not racially unified like the Etruscans. They are not Etruscans, and there was no such thing as "Venetian" in this sense. They are made up of Lombards and the Veneti. A Florentine would say "Yes, we are Etruscans, indeed!" But Venice is based on the fact that many different cultures came together and worked together to make something out of a very marginal territory. The appreciation of Venice went beyond getting to know the monuments. We were impressed by how things could exist simultaneously, coincidentally, in space.

For example, one of the students in the Venice studio made us aware of the musical dimension of the city which is called polyphony. In a certain sense the music of Saint Mark's was set by its geometries in that it had two choirs. Sound could come from two places at once, bounce around and then enter the whole space. Vivaldi in particular, Monteverdi and others, made music to match the multiple voices that could be going around at the same time. And when you are in those churches, between the sunlight coming in and the incense—both the smell and the visibility of the smoke—and the sound coming at you—the sun

Venice during Carnival, 1994.

THE TALE OF THE LIBRARIAN, SERLIO, AND THE NEXT LYRIC THEATRE

The library is to be founded at the spatial crossroads of three tenacious elements: the natural preconditions of mountain and spring, the proscriptive urban imposition of the grid, and finally, the cosmological abstraction of the oval.

One ancient map indicates that this settlement's origin is magically contained within the shaman's sixteen square grid. Yet other cartographers celebrate the hemispherical coincidence of the VPI drill field as the true center of the Universe...

Blacksburg in 1853, from the Lewis Miller sketchbook.

...but it should be noted that even today there are venerable citizens who place little faith in such papery abstractions. They whisper insistently that the oblique mountains and circuitous springs have always truly been at the essence of this place, long before mapmakers threatened to flatten their kaleidoscopic presence...

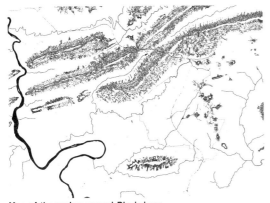

Map of the region around Blacksburg.

comes in obliquely through the high windows above—the incense from below—the sound pops out and bounces around you. You cannot help but be affected by a condition that is not just singular and straightforward but has multiple things happening at a very intense level at the same time. I think it is about a civic space that is, indeed, noisy. There are many voices there, standing for many conditions.

The curiosity of the Venetians towards the tourists was affirmed by these pictures we saw by Pietro Longhi, painted in the 1780s. He painted Venetians looking at Turks, Venetians looking at Africans, Venetians looking at Orientals—and the foreigners looking back at them. He holds this whole conversation—"Who is the stranger?" The city is used as a place of people engaging one another and trespassing on spaces, absorbing one another. The issue of observation, engagement and trespassing is the theme of the design studio we're doing now.

I think that when citizens and foreigners alike begin to cross over one another's turf, they begin to share something and a civil agenda comes out of it. There are so many lines on the street in Venice. Professor di Thiene showed us that the pavement isn't just made up of black stones, but actually has lines of white stones running at lots of different angles. We couldn't figure out why. He said that they were property lines. When you have a church on one side and perpendicular to that is a house—how do you divide whose is whose? What they've done is drawn an oblique line, so the house gets a bit of a triangle. Just walking around, you constantly had to trespass on the residential territory to get to the civic. The city, we saw, is filled with all these strange picturesque lines, but they are very real lines and very precise, recording these histories.

You know, there is this issue of how we come as strangers to a place—as architects. We come as trespassers in certain ways, and what fictions we write or extrapolate from seeing those fragments or ruins are very important, not for their truthfulness or their accuracy, but because they spur the imagination. We could have said, "We are going to be contextual and do critical regionalism," as if we were familiar citizens. But it is also intriguing to say here is a stranger coming from afar and reading it a different way. As the "other" coming to Venice we found it to be an incredible territory—because it doesn't fit! It's messy that way...noisy...the whole thing is falling apart. So we took this issue on, not to fit so easily, because we were not from there. We tried to be sympathetic, but we thought that the civil agenda should be somewhat strained.

THE BLACKSBURG PROJECT

It seems in all your work, both in your practice and in the studios you teach, you are interested in the representation of multiple histories. That is, you look to the many myths and origins of a place as the basis of an architectural narrative. What were some of the histories or myths you found in Blacksburg, and how did they inform your design for the library competition?

When we started the Blacksburg competition we read the available material on Blacksburg and I was very much interested in its origins. A very important question for us was how could one take a site and recall, re-connect, or make visible the essence of a natural and man-made history. We tried very hard to record aspects of the city that are there now, including things that might be hidden. There was this very important stream that flowed below the site that we uncovered and used to define one edge of the site. We also kept an existing grove of trees. From another period there is this house, the most famous house in town...it has five chimneys and seven gables. We found ourselves always talking about the scale of these domestic monuments. But we didn't recreate the house. Instead we organized the central reading room to be a phenomenal transformation of those seven gables, which would recall that other monument. So there are these preconditions of the house, and the natural history of the stream and grove...and I should also say the mountains are part of that roofing, as well as the view of the mountains from one side.

We also looked to the campus of the Virginia Polytechnic Institute on the other side of town. VPI doesn't have a "lawn", but this elliptical drill field, which we recalled as a fragment in the new civic space. We figured here was a significant form where people gather—to drill, which is to do something routine, to go through known paces. But it's also a place where you can observe. We conceived of the civic space adjoining the library by including a fragment of the drill field. So the site plan we developed was really a record of these natural and architectural histories, these preconditions.

And then there is this last thing we found, the most recent history—two theatrical masks of comedy and tragedy, which we found in one of the books on Blacksburg. It spoke about the history of the local theater which over many years had burned down several times, but they had saved these masks. We thought this issue of theater was critical to our urban agenda. We set up our site, which was adjacent to the police station and the city hall, so that there might be three

...still others insist that Five Chimneys which begat Five Gables and an assortment of Oddly Numbered Porches serve as the only proper measure of this town's architecture (school children learn that within the roof structure of the new reading room lies the model and measure of these historic houses)...

The Alexander Black House, built 1892.

...piers encircle the edge of this new "Lyric Theatre" in celebration of comedy and tragedy. These ancient concrete heads are made into bronze fountains which spew new life into ancient springs recovered from the obscuring landscape of previous generations...

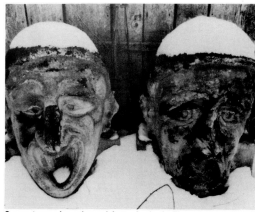
Concrete masks salvaged from the Lyric Theatre.

...recently in this century, the last map was issued when the current Town Hall, the Police Station, and a converted lumber warehouse, now called the Library by some, were located self-consciously south of Main Street to initiate this civic precinct. Here the Librarian will mount his podium and greet the Police Chief to the West. Then they turn North to wave to the Mayor: three notably humble points defining the edge of this collective stadium...

Giorgione, The Altarpiece of Castelfranco.

..but a newcomer to this town finds all the maps insufficient. Only a stranger might speculate why Main Street is now challenged by Draper Road. Issues of front, back, and flank skirt the new proscenium. Draper becomes the ambiguous territory, the condensation of a natural leitmotif, original dwellings, and civic institutions. Serlio has been waiting in the wings for years now, and awaits the challenge of such coincidental territories.

Opposite left: Model of library; side, front, and back.
Opposite right: Serlio's stagesets; tragic, comic, and satyric.

significant actors in the life of the community. One would be the mayor. One would be the police chief, and one might be the librarian. People usually think of a librarian as someone who only sits behind a desk, a humble, "bookish" figure. But we thought the keeper of the book was an extraordinarily important player in society, and since the rare book collection, the archives of the local history, would be kept there we thought she or he would be extremely important for re-telling the history of this place. So we projected three little stages or pope's balconies to provide individual places where on special holidays each of them might speak. And on special days people could gather and be congested in a place where there might be a number of people speaking. In some ways it would operate like Piazza S. Marco, where the patriarch of the church has a position to speak from, and the Doge, and the actors on their temporary stagesets. There's this deliberate theatricality. I believe that cities should be able to turn to architecture as something intentionally scenographic.

I am very sensitive to this issue. At a certain point when I was in school, this is almost thirty years ago, a juror said to me, "You're a stage set designer, not an architect." But it occurs to me that, indeed, setting up the opportunity for something larger than life or extraordinary is very important. The ideas we put into the Blacksburg project actually recall this agenda of setting up a very artificial condition—a series of fragmented stage sets or facades.

In other projects and in your studio you frequently refer to Serlio's three types of stage sets—the tragic, the comic, and the satyric. In formal terms, how have these three types influenced your design for the Blacksburg library?

If you look at the bar building on the side by the police station it is highly repetitive, both in the human scaled reading niches as well as the rhythm of the stacks. It has a very rational side which deals with the storage of stacks of books...the systematic organization of books. If tragedy is related to the obsession of reason, this side is tragic—it's intentionally rational and accessible. The front, I would say, is comic. That is, it is circumstantial and highly dynamic in terms of its forms. The satyric side, I think, is where the building engages the woods and it looks like it's either being built up or falling apart. It is akin, I believe, to a natural process of incremental construction.

In many respects your design for the library is very modern, in its materials and

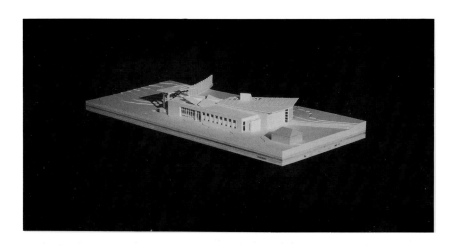

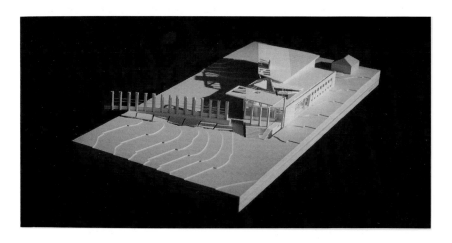

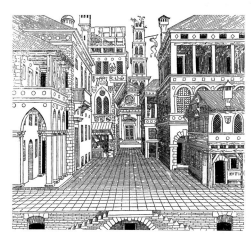

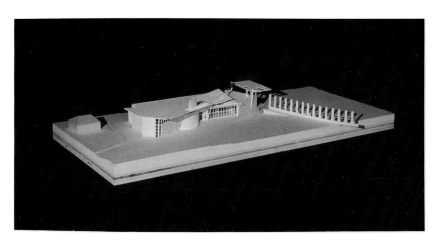

Only here can fiction and non-fiction seem naturally at home under one roof--where the elderly find the warmth of the sun and children bloom in the shadowy caves of their imaginations.

View of library interior, children' collection.

formal language, yet your renderings are filled with these classical figures. It seems curious.

We thought it extremely important that in a competition for a public building we have many figures. We wanted to capture the jury's attention, but more important, we wanted to have figures in it that would suggest a gathering. Also, these figures have costumes, like putting on something a little more than what is necessary.

In these lean times one must always question doing what seems unnecessary. But I'm not willing to give up the fact that there needs to be something magical, that you save up for a tiny bit of gold leaf, and have something sparkle. I think there may be an agenda, a civil agenda, where a precious material is used, whether it be a tiny gold ball on top of a flag pole...or the way the Russians

View of library interior, garden entry.

covered their onion domes with gold leaf to catch the light. And I would hate that present economic conditions would not permit us the civil agenda of precious materials, or adornment. So the figures are in costume and they're adorned and strangely out of place.

So far we've talked about your intentions for a civil architecture and the role architecture can play in the political and cultural life of people. In more explicit terms I'd like to broach the subject of the city, which might be the greater goal of architecture, of your architecture at least. What are your intentions for the city? How would you define the city?

Perhaps the definition of the city has to be tied into a definition of the "other" in the city. The city, some have argued, is the place where politics occurs. Ken

Frampton, I believe, in a lecture said that agriculture was the pre-requisite to culture—culture occurs within the city. When you have a surplus of agriculture, you store it in the city. The city then begins to have a life other than sheer necessity. But it's also the crossroads where the citizen and the stranger encounter one another. The city might be a place where curiosity or amusement, in a very profound sense, can occur. When somebody from some other place actually passes through the walls and is observed, it makes you aware of another condition. But I don't have an easy definition yet, nor am I really seeking one.

Perhaps another way of talking about the city is to compare it to something that is not quite a city, which in our American experience, arguably, is the suburb. By suburb I mean this movement toward a pastoral ideal, the middle landscape, a condition where everybody's isolated from each other physically and everyone gets about by car. You've talked about chance encounters or encounters with strangers. In the suburbs that doesn't happen that often, not firsthand.

Because Venice is a pedestrian city, one can't help but encounter people in a very close way given the narrow streets, both the tourists and the inhabitants. It is the nature of that place to accommodate the interaction of the stranger and the citizen. And one can in a very short time get out to the country, the rural condition, and see huge ancient trees, and furrowed ground. As we traveled outside of Venice we saw that every inch of the landscape was of an agricultural condition. Every inch was productive. And we thought it was fantastic that we lived in a city of great density, encountering strangers, etcetera, but the things that sustained us, in terms of food and stone quarries were not so far away. The pre-requisite for the city, the pre-requisite for the discussion was this distinction between an urban and a rural condition.

In America, one does not get contact with that natural condition so immediately. Maybe I can bring in my experience having lived in Houston, which is a very self-consciously American city. Houston is really a collection of dozens of community shopping centers surrounded by houses—each with one live oak tree and the requisite Spanish Moss. In the space between the houses is this dimension of the automobile—the very vehicle that allows them to sustain that low density. It is an incredible city, the fourth largest in the United States, but it is all of a suburban condition. There are not even porches on the houses because there's no pretense of meeting somebody in an ambiguous place—half in, half out.

Contained within the plan of The Library one might decipher the section of its situation, its topographies, its numerous meters, and its fragmented original centers.

In the midst of this civic facility, the gabled territory of Five Chimneys and the equally kaleidescopic mountains re-establish these two dimensions of this town in the spatial middleground of four prismatic reading rooms.

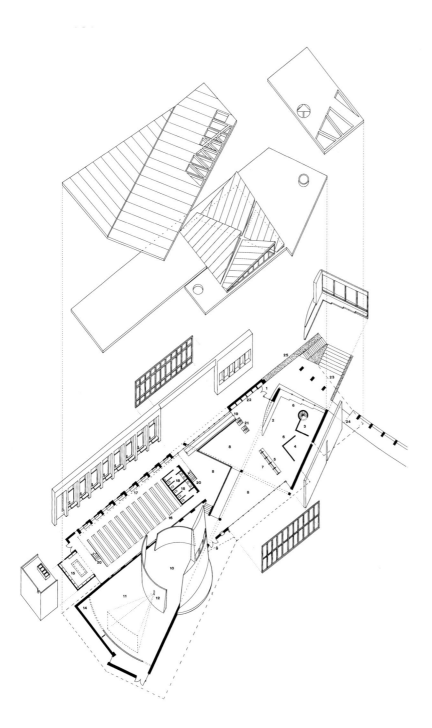

The Blacksburg Library. Exploded Axonometric.

This new town center aspires to the dream of Brunelleschi; to create one urban room for all the citizens of the region to gather in celebration of their origins. Fragments of the VPI drill field move finally after centuries of separation into a layered relationship engaging the shaman's original sixteen square grid. Fragments of this collective geometry double the Police Station and Library providing additional facilities as well as belvedere spaces from which to address the mountainous dimension of this context. Main Street is to be densified in the most conventional manner. A block away to the south, re-oriented to the power of Nature this new urban theatre will encompass citizens and students, natural resources and historic artifacts in the spirit of the Ultimate Palimpsest. The Librarian is the gate keeper and stage manager of this urban condition re-situated within the theatres of the American Wilderness.

PROJECT CREDITS

Project Team:
David Ackerman, Joe Atkins, Sam Holloway, John Farmer, David Puckett, Peter Waldman, Seth Warner.

FIGURE CREDITS

Frontis Photo by Paolo Salviati, 1890. Courtesy of Buffalo Bill Historical Center, Cody, WY.
1,2 Photo by Kirsten Stadheim.
3 Courtesy of the Abbey Aldrich Rockefeller Folk Art Center, Williamsburg, Virginia.
4,6 *Town Architecture*, Donna Dunay, ed. (Blacksburg: Virginia Polytechnic Institute and State University)
5 Courtesy Virginia Polytechnic Institute and State University, Special Collections, Blacksburg, VA.
7 Giorgione, Altarpiece of Castelfranco, c. 1504.
11-13 Sebastiano Serlio, *The Five Books of Architecture*.

All drawings and photographs of the Blacksburg project courtesy of the author.

And I find that it is very difficult to establish a civil agenda in a place where people drive from parking lot to parking lot and don't have to walk back and forth across common ground every day to pick up their bread or go to work. There are very few places that we use as public space on a daily basis. In contemporary life people don't gather, or hardly ever gather. We'd much rather sit around televisions and witness people doing things than doing things ourselves. We seem to spend so much time at home. You don't even need to go any place to work any more because of what communications and technology allow. Suburbia is such an idealized kind of thing that you have a little bit of nature and a little bit of house, and you can do almost every thing within your own precinct. You don't have to go anywhere. You don't have to go regularly. You are not part of a civil space. You don't have a need for it.

If I were to give a definition of the city, and if one position is focussed on politics, then I would also insist that the city also provide landscapes for the imagination, and magic. The city can be scary as a labyrinth, for in those noisy and congested places you might just encounter a Minotaur. Unless there is the possibility of first impressions, there can be no history of the future, that is, if everything is known or predictable. So the city, I think, is the very nurturing and risky place which permits the survival of the imagination.

The city I'm interested in, as opposed to a wholly knowable and resolved city, concerns them all: the tragic, the comic, and the satyric. Serlio is my urban agenda. It's probably in the Serlio condition, of the three conditions existing simultaneously that I would ground the city—in the rational, in the circumstantial, and in the satyric. And of the three, if you want me to be precise, the satyric is the thing that is most neglected. It is in the realm of the satyric where man meets nature, where one could be extraordinarily imaginative.

Opposite: View of site model.

FEAR OF ARCHITECTURE:
THE ARCHITECT'S ROLE IN THE DECLINE OF AMERICAN URBANISM

MARK SCHIMMENTI

Mark Schimmenti is Associate
Professor of Architecture at The
University of Virginia School of
Architecture where he teaches
design and contemporary
American urbanism.

Critical texts on American urbanism from Jane Jacobs in *Death and Life of Great American Cities* to the recent work *The Geography of Nowhere* by James Kunstler have described the success and failure of architecture's role in the formation of the civic realm. In the exemplary cases, a positive urban fabric is defined by a network of public spaces including a strong civic realm. Federal Washington and Annapolis are just such examples due to their well defined civic realms which provide meaningful environments to resident and visitor alike. Despite convincing arguments and continual deference to good existing models, the built environment is an increasingly unattractive and unpleasant place to conduct civic activities. Architecture as a civic art giving form to the civic realm rarely occurs in late twentieth century development in America. In a recent report, HUD's Office of Community Planning and Development pointed out the painfully apparent condition that society's ills can be directly linked to the quality of our built environment; "Current patterns of city building are unsustainable ... and breed poverty and fear." [1]

People spend the majority of their time in places which are determined, for the most part, without architects or architectural criteria. The role of the architect has been reduced to the task of building design within a set of rules that are established by others such as bankers and planners. The architectural profession, however, rarely takes an active role in the processes that shape neighborhoods, towns and cities. This lack of participation in contemporary society has allowed sprawl to replace the civic environment. Society needs architects who are concerned with the role of architecture in the community and with the fostering of the civic environment. To the point: if the civic realm is defined by building——and architecture is the art of building——and architects practice architecture——then architects are responsible for the definition of the civic realm.

Why do most architects ignore their social responsibility? What follows is the proposition that architects are less than effective in the civic realm because they are preoccupied with other concerns. In choosing to occupy their thoughts and actions with these other issues, they exhibit a phobia of a socially responsible architecture.

Pennsylvania Avenue, Washington, D.C.

PROBABLE CAUSE

The call for professional leadership and expertise seems to come from everywhere. It comes over the evening news when neighborhoods cry for justice and peace. It comes from the shopping mall when young people attempt to grow up amid a world limited to crass commercialization. It comes from the inner-city as people grow up on street corners among economic and social poverty with little or no community guidance. It comes from the citizen groups asking for community integrity. It comes from a landscape bludgeoned into the forms and uses that are sprawl. To answer this call is to take the first step toward restoring architecture to a significant place in the body politic.

Why does the profession of architecture ignore these voices? Those who signal the trends in architecture—whether practitioner, professor, student, or layperson—seem unwilling to stop and listen to these cries.[2] One opinion professes, in absolute terms, that it is unimportant to address society's issues and to ask only shows ignorance. Another stance is that all this is necessary if architecture is to progress into the 21st century. Yet another position points out that architects have no control over where they are going and must swim with the current in order to survive. This impatience manifests itself in the modern psyche as stated by Kierkegaard. "To what shall we compare the conceit of modernity that hungers for instant recognition prior to any actual achievement? The present is the age of anticipation when even recognition is received in advance. No one is satisfied with doing something definite, every one wants to feel flattered by reflection of the illusion of having discovered at the very least a new continent."[3]

The conditions illustrated in the following text share the attitude that the memory of civic architecture and not the refined knowledge of the civic realm drives contemporary endeavors. What the ancient Greeks assumed to be a lifetime task, our age, however, presumes to be able to figure out before graduation.[4] It was assumed in the time of the Greeks that memory could not be followed with conviction, and knowing is not acquired in either days, weeks, months, or years. As Faulkner wrote in his attempt to illustrate a flawed personality within a seriously flawed society, "Memory believes before knowing remembers. Believes longer than recollects, longer than knowing even wonders."[5]

For the Greeks, it was a sign of urbanity and culture that one could be satisfied working within architecture; it was very odd to consider the path beyond. Contemporary architects do not spend enough time and energy trying to understand their work as civic art as opposed to personal art, and their responsibility to society through architectural means. Too many architects limit the possibilities of architecture by addressing a singular, or a severely limited palate of issues.[6] As a result, they on memory for guidance and direction rather than gaining direction from knowing the role of architecture in society.

FEAR

Most architects dwell within a closed village that pays little or no attention to the larger issues of society. Because the world of architects is not involved with the issues that shape the larger world, factors which determine the built environment today rarely deal with issues of the civic realm. What causes this condition to prevail in our studios and offices? The answer lies deep within the attitudes that shape the idea of architecture both as an academic and a professional pursuit. The architect's phobia of the primary responsibility of the profession, service to society, causes him or her to seek asylum within one or more of the following conditions. Three dominant conditions together make up the Fear of Architecture.

View of Annapolis.

Tyson's Corner.

FEAR OF ARCHITECTURE CONDITION 1. (FOA1)

"Architecture should be a radical, cutting edge art form and is best expressed on a revolutionary platform."

or

The Discreet Fear of the Avant Garde

The work resulting from this attitude usually wears its radical content as a formalistic medal. The urge to be avant garde pervades all thought: every other issue becomes subservient. The avant garde, which fearlessly forges forward into a future, dreads things mundane, pedestrian, or practical entering the architectural equation.

FoA1 has been illustrated, and rewarded, in the architectural periodicals for some years. It first appeared in the fourteenth annual Progressive Architecture design awards 25 years ago. Despite a strongly split jury, Venturi and Rauch were chosen to receive an Award and two Citations.[6] Compared to the other honored projects , the Venturi and Rauch work was very different. The Frug House, named after a dance craze of the time, was a small pool house appearing in the magazine as a simple chip-board model and accompanied by economic line drawings. While the Venturi and Rauch work was praised for being "inclusive rather than exclusive" and generally lauded for its effort to respond to cultural issues, it becomes apparent that the Award was based on the project's radical content. Another Venturi and Rauch project receiving a lesser prize, a civic center for Canton, Ohio, had more program, carried out its design in the civic realm, and addressed more issues than the private Frug House.[7] The selection of this "place for children's parties"[8] for an Award prompted one juror to comment, "I don't care whether the Frug House people love it or not. What bothers me is that this magazine is going to be coming out in January and every young kid is going to be turning the pages and saying 'Wow, this is it this year!' "[9]

This fascination with an architecture rooted in radical content grew into a preoccupation in the 1970s. Superstudio and Archigram emerged during this period as serious contenders for the attention of younger architects bored with the rigors of Mies, Rowe, and Wittkower. This media based revolution came to a head with the Shinkenchiku Residential Design Competition of 1975.[10] This competition historically called for international solutions to mass housing: a particularly important concern in postwar Japan. Arata Isozaki was judge for the 1975 competition which he titled "House for a Superstar." The winning entry, a house for Raquel Welch, was selected for first prize because of its radical content, yet, it was never meant to exist. In Mr. Isozaki's words, "the work is excellent because it depicts the mechanism whereby a fictitious residence is created."[11] Ultimately, this was a reward for a radical gesture rather than for an architectural solution.

In 1981 the Institute for Architecture and Urban Studies sponsored a competition for architects under the age of 35. The competition asked for solutions to the poorly defined traffic snarl of Columbus Circle in New York. The entry that was selected for first place and installed was a radical gesture: a grid of traffic cones. Design solutions, such as the proposal by Frederic Schwartz, that proposed a better definition of Columbus Circle were all but ignored. The IAUS and its founders promoted FoA1 and gave legitimacy to an architecture of radical gesture that ignored real issues. According to Alberti, architecture is a built (or at least a buildable) idea based on the needs of society. Architecture according to those who dwell within FoA1 is a radical gesture for the enjoyment of the initiated.

The present form of this condition, whatever it is, will eventually wear itself out like so many "hot items" that have gone before. The next "new" architecture will replace the current model only to be replaced with another as soon as boredom sets in. If, as Kierkegaard says, boredom is the root of all evil, then we may be bored ad infinitum. Following Kierkegaard; "It is very curious that boredom, which

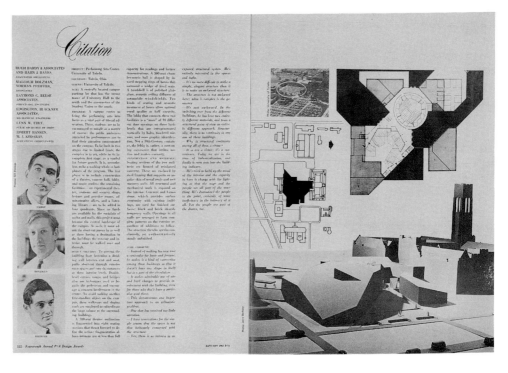

Top: 1967 *Progressive Architecture* Citation - Performing Arts Center, University of Toronto by Hugh Hardy & Associates and Hahn & Hayes.
Bottom right: 1967 *Progressive Architecture Award*, Frug House by Venturi, Scott Brown and Associates.
Bottom left: North Canton City Hall by Venturi and Rauch.

itself has such a calm and sedate nature, can have such a capacity to initiate motion. The effect that boredom brings about is absolutely magical, but this effect is not one of attraction but of repulsion."[13]

How does one stop the cycle of subjugation to FoA1? Can boredom be avoided? Success lies in the suppression of radical content as a major component and critical measure of architectural work. In other words, the definition of architectural form should not be driven by boredom but by a larger view. This larger view exists from working within the issues as defined by society, not from the memory of constructs created within the world of architecture. This tendency, which may now be considered a tradition in most schools of architecture, could easily be stopped by an architecture that responds positively to important social issues

Top: The Walking City by Archigram.
Bottom: Il Monumento Continuo, 1969, by Superstudio.

Top: Raquel Welch House by Tom Heneghan.
Bottom left: Columbus Circle Competition Entry by Frederic Schwartz.
Bottom right: Columbus Circle Competition Installation by Elizabeth Diller.

FEAR OF ARCHITECTURE CONDITION 2 (FOA2)

"Architecture and its validity can be judged best in reference to the idea of the modern condition and architectural design's ability to exhibit change and progress."

or

The Overt Fear of the Modernist Mind.

FoA2 has fostered architecture and architectural ideas derived from either a formal determinism steeped in abstraction or an envy of achievements in other fields such as science, industrial design, linguistics, environmental engineering and so on. To satisfy a perceived necessity for architecture to be "of-its-time", theories and ideas from outside the body of architectural knowledge supplanted time-proven, society-driven issues including the sense of place, civic art, and so on.

While FoA2 searches for the elusive "spirit of the age", it does so within a more limited world view than that associated with the Zeitgeist as described in the German-Swiss art historical tradition. FoA2 tries to translate trends into form and calls this a movement, while the reverse is true for the Zeitgeist assessment of architectural form in history.[14] The call for an architecture 'appropriate to this day and age' asks for what is valuable only to the standards of the moment it is built. Architecture under FoA2 must always be 'new' and by reference architecture can and must be improved. Such an architecture has been alluded to since Hegel. It is the main argument in Le Corbusier's call to arms as outlined in *Towards a New Architecture*.

Following Viollet-le-Duc and into the early part of the 20th century, we find a strong and logical case being made against "architect's architecture" and for the belief that architectural works are always determined by outside forces. For example, Greek temples were explained under the Zeitgeist in terms of the limitations of the materials and the effect this had on the form rather than as deliberate compositions based on traditional forms and rules. The essential form of the temple happened as a result of the methods and materials of ancient building. The importance of architectural composition and tradition were inessential to the architecture of the temple. In turn, proper contemporary architecture would happen if modern technologies inform the composition. Such ideas rest comfortably within the art-historical method for the critique of architecture championed by Hegel and his followers that gave theoretical justification to the Modern Movement, a method that, in the writings of critics like Pevsner and Giedion, proposed an architecture of its time and judged all contemporary architectural work on the expression of the idea of modernity.

Buildings unavoidably belong to the times and places in which they are built. It is reductionist to think that the principle content of a building is the Zeitgeist. Architecture naturally expresses the spirit-of-the-age. The issue is not whether the concerns of technology or intellectual thought should affect architecture, but that architecture itself should not be isolated from issues of civic importance.

The pioneers of the Modern Movement preached their chosen type of architecture "...as an inescapable natural and moral commitment... ."[15] However, Watkin explains, the theoretical base for this belief was wholly inarticulate, relied heavily on rhetoric that could endure a wide-range of interpretation, and was at best loose and vacuous. By imparting a mystical quality to the 20th century process of design, Le Corbusier undermined and discredited architecture's self-referential qualities. Here follows an example from *Towards a New Architecture* :

Delage. Front-Wheel Brake: This precision, this cleanness in execution go further back than our re-born mechanical sense. Phidias felt this way: the entablature of the Parthenon is a witness. So did the Egyptians when they polished the Pyramids. This at a time when Euclid and Pythagoras dictated to their contemporaries. [16]

The measure one is expected to uphold in FoA2 is the modern conception of progress as improvement. This notion of progress "rests on the belief that human wants are insatiable, that new wants appear as soon as old ones are satisfied and that steadily rising levels of comfort will lead to an infinite expansion."[17] While this may constitute a suitable critical framework for a new technological process or product, it is wholly inadequate as a measure of architecture. The demands of society, for electronic products or for medical science for example, are demonstrable. A faster computer marks progress in electronics. A human want for a faster way to do work is satisfied. A new, life-saving, medical technique moves the health profession forward. Architecture, the art of building and the definer of the civic realm, cannot demonstrate progress as defined above. For example, a house solely designed as a machine for living in cannot address the issues of society as a civic body. The house can be fascinating, inventive, and intellectually provocative as a construct, a built diagram of an idea, and not address the social criteria for architecture. Accordingly, the house as a "machine for living in" would not be architecture nor would it represent architectural progress.

Piano & Rogers, Lloyd's of London.

Viollet-le-Duc, Interior of Assembly Hall.

From *Towards a New Architecture*.

FEAR OF ARCHITECTURE CONDITION 3 (FOA3)

"Architecture is impossible today."

or

The Indiscreet Fear of the Rear Guard.

FoA3 subsists within both the discrete fear that possesses the avant garde and the overt fear inherent in the modernist mind. The avant garde proudly builds a non-architecture and the modernist mind drives the wheels of a "new" architecture. Both a non-architecture and a "new" architecture are reactionary products to the impossibility of building an architecture of the civic realm. In the case of FoA1 and FoA2 the proponents choose not to address society's need for a civic realm and are driven mostly by the issues set forth earlier in this paper. However, it is the prevalence of FoA3 in professional practice that affects the built environment, and thus society and the civic realm, most directly. It is within the offices of architects that FoA3 truly exists.

Architecture has become impossible for today's practitioners for two main reasons: one, the architect has become so consumed with the task of running an office that little or no time or energy is available to address the issues of the civic realm, and two, current building practice is almost totally controlled by a fragmented and isolated set of conditions from which the architect is excluded. In the former, the practicing professional gives up on architecture and in the latter he or she is confronted with program and standards that almost never address the civic realm.

For this group, architecture is so difficult, given the multitude of issues that confront any project, that it is unrealistic to expect anything other than the mediocre. Issues of civic importance are rarely addressed in any other than a cursory fashion. Once an architectural office has confronted the rules and regulations of building, the marketing strategies and value engineering of the client, the negotiations of the planning officials, the land-use codes and the programming models enforced by the financiers, very little time or energy is available to work out the architecture's role in society.

The models for an American urbanism that has a strong civic realm, such as in Federal Washington or Annapolis, are now illegal. They could not be built today under current rules and regulations; rules and regulations which have been made during the architect's absence from the processes that form public policy. The design of suburbia, and the sprawl around it, is built exactly to these bylaws. Sprawl, and all of its problems, is due, in large part, to the profession's lack of involvement in the processes that shape the built world. While the forefront of profession fiddled around with the non-issues of FoA1 and FoA2 and the rear guard of FoA3 was too busy to care, others wrote the policy that makes architecture, and the civic realm, impossible for society. The Edge Cities that define much of the building of the past decade are emblematic of the architect's absence from the determination of the civic realm.

Our world as we build it.

So if:

The civic realm is defined by building.

The quality of the civic realm is directly related to the quality of the buildings. The conditions that make up the Fear of Architecture have shifted the task of building from the issues that would form a civic realm of great quality. Buildings must better define our world.

and

Architecture is the art of building.

A reconciliation between construction and architecture will produce more satisfying buildings. In the best examples, radical content is absent, the design is confidently architectural, and no excuse exists in place of design excellence. Good architecture absorbs the best of its time into the design. Doing this well can be as satisfying as, and is more challenging than, striking a radical referential position, thereby avoiding measuring achievement by the extent to which a design is submerged, and is the result of issues which are non-architectural. If architecture were the art of building within society, our world would be better defined.

and

Architects practice architecture.

If the architects of our shopping malls, our "Edge Cities", and our strip malls could pull their heads out of the sand and stand up for the role of the profession as leaders of the construction of our world we would be well on our way to breaking the third leg of this condition of fear. If those who do the hard work of making civic art possible were supported by the academics and theoreticians we would be well on our way to activating larger sectors of the architectural world. Those operating in the political world are the ones making the decisions that shape the built environment. Architects must become politically active in order to return the act of building to its proper place in the definition of the civic realm. If architects would practice architecture, the art of building within society, our world would be better defined.

then

Architects are responsible for the definition of the civic realm.

If the civic realm is to be defined and produced by architects, first there must be a desire to address issues within society. The institutions that educate and organize architects need to show the way to achieving this goal. This should start in the universities. By rejecting the tripartite conditions that make up "Fear of Architecture," our education system will better prepare architects to address issues and generate architecture from a stance critical of short-term gratification. Architects would value the leadership role in defining the process of building communities if this potential role were given importance and guidance in the pedagogy of the architectural education. The profession would impart value to the architect as conductor of the civic realm by a conscious shift toward this direction. So, in time, architects and architecture can and will define the political life of our cities.

NOTES

1 Office of Community Planning and Development, HUD, *Vision/Reality: strategies for community change*, HUD-1446-CPD, March 1994.

2 Soren Kierkegaard, *Fear and Trembling* (Princeton: Princeton University Press, 1983), 5-8. Kierkegaard reflects on the philosophers who seem "unwilling to stop and listen."

3 Thomas C. Oden, *Parables of Kierkegaard* (Princeton: Princeton University Press, 1978), 72.

4 Kierkegaard, 6.

5 William Faulkner, *Light in August* (New York: Random House, 1932), 88.

6 As of this writing architectural education seems to be in an act of retrenchment behind the front lines of architectonics. The so-called poetics of construction and "truth in materials" are quickly taking hold again. This is apparently a reaction to the anti-architectonics of Post-Modern and Deconstructionist work. Although this retro-rationalism may promote craft, it, like Post-Modernism and Deconstruction, has no social component. Architecture without a social agenda will pass to the next fad quickly because its values are shallow.

7-9 *Progressive Architecture*, January 1967, 144-148.

10 Ironically, the awarding of the Frug House for its shock value promoted the idea of radical content in the design studios. The real message of inclusive, useful, and meaningful architecture promoted by Robert Venturi and Denise Scott Brown was mostly ignored. The influence of the urban design work of Scott Brown and Venturi on what has been called the New Urbanism is yet to be valued as well.

11,12 *Japan Architect*, February 1976, 20-23.

13 Kierkegaard, *Either/Or*, Volume 1, "The Rotation Method: a venture in a theory of social prudence." (Princeton: Princeton University Press, 1987), 281-300.

14 David Watkin, *Morality and Architecture* (Oxford: Clarendon Press, 1977).

15 Watkin, 38.

16 Le Corbusier, *Towards a New Architecture* (Dover, 1986), 129.

17 C. Lasch, *The True and Only Heaven* (New York: Norton, 1991).

18 Leon Krier, "The Blind Spot", *Architectural Design*, Vol. 48, No. 4, 1978, 119-221. After making a case for architecture as the art of building Mr. Krier states on page 119: "... if architecture is essentially an intellectual discipline it cannot ... free itself from its subject and origin: building."

19 Robert Jan. van Pelt and C. W. Westfall, *Architectural Principles in the Age of Historicism* (New Haven: Yale University Press, 1991), 46-48. The term political as used in this paper refers to what C. W. Westfall defines as the *political life* and its relationship to the *idea* of the city.

FIGURE CREDITS

Frontis Photo by Sallah Baloch.

1 Photo by Randi Stone.

2 Photo by Sallah Baloch.

3,5 Progressive Architecture, January 1967.

4 Courtesy Venturi, Scott Brown and Associates.

6 *Archigram* (London: Studio Vista Publishers, 1972).

7 *Superstudio, 1966-1982, Storie, figure, architettura* (Milan: Electa Editrice,1982).

8 *Japan Architect*, Feb. 1976.

9 Courtesy Frederic Schwartz, AIA.

10,16 Photo by Author.

11 Photo by Richard Bryant, Deyan Sudjic, *Norman Foster, Richard Rogers, James Stirling, New directions in British Architecture* (London: Thames and Hudson Inc., 1987).

12 M.F. Hearn, Ed., *The Architectural Theory of Viollet-le-Duc: readings and commentary* (Cambridge: MIT Press, 1990).

13 ©1995 Artists Rights Society (ARS), New York / SPADEM, Paris.

14-15,17 Photo by Sallah Baloch.

THE CLASSICAL AMERICAN CITY IN IMAGE AND IN CHICAGO

CARROLL WILLIAM WESTFALL

Carroll William Westfall is Professor of Architectural History at the University of Virginia and is co-author of *Architectural Principles in the Age of Historicism*.

Since we see that every city is some sort of partnership, and that every partnership is constituted for the sake of some good (for everyone does everything for the sake of what is held to be good), it is clear that all partnerships aim at some good, and that the partnership that is most authoritative of all and embraces all the others does so particularly, and aims at the most authoritative good of all. This is what is called the city or the political partnership.

Aristotle, *Politics*, I, i (1252a), Carnes Lord trans.

But perhaps it will seem wonderful to inexperienced persons that human nature can master and hold in recollection so large a number of subjects. When, however, it is perceived that all studies are related to one another and have points of contact, they will easily believe it can happen. For a general education is put together like one body from its members.

Vitruvius, *Ten Books on Architecture*, I, i, 12, Frand Granger trans.

For just as the body is one and has many members, and all the members of the body, though many, are one body, so it is with Christ. For in the one Spirit we were all baptized into one body —Jews or Greeks, slaves or free— and we were all made to drink of one Spirit.

I Cor. 12: 12-13.

Chicago. Proposed boulevard to connect the north and south sides of the river.

In the West, before life was transformed over the last few hundred years, the world was known as a stable place with the city well-established within it. Change, whether in things, thoughts, or actions, occurred against a background of continuity, and the word modern referred simply to their newest form. The new, the modern, was not valued for its own sake but only insofar as it allowed a clearer knowledge of what people knew to be true or as it improved upon things as they were. The old and the new, the ancient and the modern mingled with one another. Then, history was a story told about a world that still existed and about things that might still happen, although in a different, modern form.

The rise of modernism to hegemony over the last two centuries replaced the mingling of ancient and modern with a doctrine that considered them separate, that pushed the ancient into the past and labeled it traditional, and that declared its events obsolete and its truths true only in particular times. By its own criteria, the claim of modernists that truth is relative casts doubts on their claim as well as on the claim they reject. Put another way: simply because the modernist view is prominent does not make it true and other views false. Similarly, because the traditional view had a longer period of preeminence is no reason for declaring it the valid one. By the modernist's criteria, the contrast between these two views of the world is an open contest.

But this is not news. The contest has been open ever since people discovered they were responsible for their actions in the world; that is, ever since the beginning of what can be called the western tradition, a tradition whose origins can be placed in the thoughts of Greeks and Hebrews in the sixth and fifth centuries BC.[1] Modernism, in this account, has its origins in the skepticism of those who confronted the claims of absolutism and assumed personal responsibility for the outcome. The price was the insecurity that comes from not being certain; the reward was freedom, the possibility of self-knowledge, and the prospect of enjoying the happiness all people have the right to pursue.

But the current form of modernism runs deeper than mere skepticism. It seeks to reject not merely the accessibility of truth, but the very possibility of its existence. In doing so it has given the individual a substitute for the effect of knowing truth. It used to be that knowing something truthful provided happiness just as acting well or perceiving the beautiful did. Once modernism did away with the possibility of the existence of truth (and of good-

ness and of beauty), it did away with happiness and substituted pleasure.

Happiness arises in an intellectual quality that can be shared. It is intensified through its presence within a community as, for example, among those brought together in communion with God, as a community of scholars in a university, or in a patriotic celebration following victory in a just war. Pleasure refers to an emotional sensation; it is a personal value that defies communication with others except at a sub-rational level where pleasure is increased by increasing the emotional stimulus, for example, by making something louder, more intense, or more defiant of nature's laws.

Modernism bans the traditional based on the mingling of the ancient and its modern commentary. Indeed, modernism accepts no contest between it and traditionalism and instead seeks war. On one side stand modernists who believe that change is more valuable than continuity and that all truth is relative to the circumstances producing instances of it. The opposing traditionalists hold that there are certain truths that take different forms in different circumstances; that acting on the basis of those truths is preferable to revelling in change for the sake of modernity; that new, modern knowledge displaces what had been accepted as settled understandings of truth; and that happiness is found in the enjoyment of new knowledge. While the modernist takes his happiness in the individualist aesthetic of the sublime, the traditionalist gains succor from participating in a community's confrontation of the skepticism that can cast the isolated individual into despair.

These observations about traditionalism and modernism provide the background to the ruminations that follow about how we might think about the history of the American city. Modernism grew out of a European experience whose most dramatic event was the French Revolution. The founding and defining event in the history of the United States was the American Revolution, which was a very different kind of event. It had more to do with an age-old traditionalism than with a developing

Panoramic view of Chicago, Currier and Ives, 1892.

modernism. The founding years of the American Republic were marked by the restoration of old, traditional, classical truths in entirely new circumstances. The modern was placed within the traditional, not in opposition to it. This placed the new nation not within modernism but within a new classicism. That is the framework of the nation that endures today. The histories of architecture and cities do not make this distinction. They treat American and continental European works, whether buildings or cities, within the same historical framework, as if the events of July 4 and July 14 arose from the same causes, addressed the same issues, and produced the same effects. What follows are thoughts about how we might write a history of the American city congruent with this premise.

II

A traditionalist history of cities and the buildings forming them, whether in America or elsewhere, would be very different from a modernist one. Under traditionalism, cities and their buildings are histories of themselves. Each new building is seen as a commentary on the older ones, providing revisions that clarify the continuity between it and its predecessors and make suggestions about what its successors might seek. The history built as the city and the commentaries accompanying it provide a dialogue between the ancients, or the physical facilities and civil ideas already extant, and the moderns who dare to think differently and to build among them, even to the extent of replacing their old buildings with new ones.

Under modernism, buildings stand outside history, denying the past and pointing only toward the future. History is left to the historians who, quite understandably, write for an audience of modernists to the total neglect of the traditionalist position. By their account, the traditional city ceased to exist when confronted with the modernist declaration of war against the past. Not only did the building of it cease, but so too was the account of its character rewritten to make the traditional past the inevitable prelude to modernism.

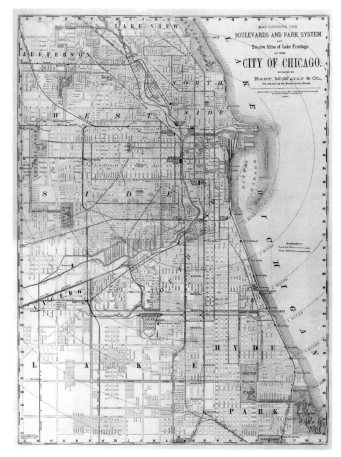

Chicago Boulevard and Park System, 1881.

Since we have all been raised as modernists, the modernist scheme of things provides us the familiar background against which we must seek to understand the unfamiliar, traditional scheme of things. Modernist histories chart the beginnings and ongoing flow of the current state of things. They see the alternative as a static tradition that the present leaves behind. Within the traditional they further distinguish a particular aspect called "classical," a term that calls for a careful gloss.

The classical is the name the precocious modernists of two centuries ago gave the products of ancient Greece and Rome, the products that had provided the high standard of achievement their successors sought to emulate. The immediate predecessors of the modernists had admired that past, perhaps none more than Winckelmann and Quatremere de Quincy, and their admiration led to the desire to emulate its achievement. There was nothing new about this. The Ionian courts of the fourth and third centuries BC had done the same, and so had others from time to time ever since—until the late eighteenth century, when for the first time there was thought to be an alternative standing quite outside that stream, an alternative that seemed equally valid if not more attractive.

None of those involved in that earlier emulation of past achievement had looked to a particular moment in the past as the best moment of the past and therefore the proper moment to bring back into the present. The past they saw was filled with a number of pasts presenting a variety of things worth knowing. Thus classicism was always a world of neoclassicism in which the neoclassical examples were simply the newer examples. There never was some moment when 'the classical' existed such that all later things were new relative to it. All classical things when they were new were neoclassical, that is, modern classical things.

Over the past century modernist scholars of the history of art and architecture have securely inserted the term neoclassicism into the canonical sequence of styles. It comes after the Rococo and before Romanticism (unless it is taken as a form of romanticism, as in Romantic Classicism). According to the rules historians use, all art objects, including buildings, have a style. A style is limited to only one appearance in history with any later uses of it being debased, imitative, false, or dishonest, and for each style there is a period just as there is a period for each style. Finally, each later authentic style is superior to those that preceded it. You can't go back; you can't stop progress.

These rules were promulgated for certain definite purposes by European positivists and their epigoni, who sought an identity for the emerging nation-states then being formed through liberation from foreign powers, and which were constituting themselves with liberal constitutions. In defining its character a nation had to define its identity through establishing not only a state, a constitution, and a language, but also a national style for the arts.

The ideas of the ancient Greeks and Romans about states, laws, a people's identity, and a destiny in history were the strongest ideas available to the scholars and statesmen of the later eighteenth and better part of the nineteenth centuries. This made neoclassicism in all areas of activity especially appealing. Starting from the assumption that history began in antiquity, styles and periods ran in a more or less direct line from the Greeks to the present: archaic, Hellenic, Hellenistic, Republican Roman, Imperial Roman, Early Christian, Carolingian, Romanesque, the Gothic diversion, the restoration known as the Renaissance, then the Baroque, the Rococo, and...and then what? Their admiration for antiquity led them to hope that the sequence had started over, this time in a new positivist, modernist form that would move quickly and inexorably to Utopia.

These sponsors of modernism have managed to build a very impressive structure atop the detritus they made of the old world. Simply note the role their inventions play in the current intellectual stock-in-trade. History was formerly a part of the humanities offering a means of cultivating the character of individuals who would play an active role in public affairs. History is now considered by many to be a social science seeking objective explanations of why things are as they are. Progress, formerly something that was measured by standards of justice and won

through exertion in the world of ethical conduct, is now thought to be assured by applying the lessons of the natural sciences to the problems of living. Art, which includes architecture, became a matter of responding to the imperatives of technology, the social sciences (for example, economics and sociology), and the autonomous artistic spirit which is generally called style. In the world constructed by the modernists, the new is more highly valued than the old merely because it is new, and value is assessed by contrasting current fashion with what it has made unfashionable.

This is a world of relativism and historicism at war with the world of enduring tradition. While traditionalists need to fight the nihilism of modernism, they embrace the invigoration of the modern. Whereas in the modernist's world each moment must be different and each different moment must be unique, in the world of traditionalism each moment is equally valued as something unique and the modern moment is especially treasured when it gives special insight into things that always have been. The modern illuminates the ancient. In the traditional world, there is an outlook upon or attitude toward the world as a whole rather than only some particular period or style in the past. In traditionalism, classicism is not a style when the word style means what modernists mean by the word. Instead, the word classical refers to the high standards that were first achieved in Greek and Roman antiquity and renewed, expanded, enlarged, deepened, and altered in a variety of modern classical forms ever since. Each current classicism, that is, every modern classicism asks for comparison with its antecedents, a comparison that is possible only if there is a similarity. In law, this similarity is in the just and ethical properties of conduct. In learning, it is in the comparison of what is known about an instance with what can be known about that instance's essence or nature. In architecture and in cities, this similarity is found in formal properties.

The formal properties make it possible to picture the traditional city. Unlike the modernist city where the new replaces the old by destroying it and where events occur in a constant flux that make it impossible for the city to retain a stable image of itself, it is always possible to produce a current image for the traditional city. It is not a fixed image but one that differs in each current moment with each current image possessing within its lineaments the image of that city that could always have been and will always be able to be produced. The potential for such an image always exists, although that image will be rendered perceptible only if someone makes a picture or builds its parts. Modern activity will thereby clarify ancient achievement. The character of this image has always been and will be the same for every traditional city: it is always made up of parts; the images of the parts are as much about the purposes the parts play in the civic whole as they are about their physical, material forms; the parts themselves are always whole and complete; and the whole is never finished, never out of date, never entirely new, and always composed of new and old parts.

It is a picture that is valid for all time and therefore it is not limited to any particular time. And it is vague—more an image than a picture even when it is drawn as a picture—because it is as much about the purpose the forms in it serve as it is about the forms themselves. The image therefore allows those who live and act in its material embodiment to understand the relationship between the current form of the place they live in and the one it has had in the past and will have in the future. To do so requires that it be a public image, an image that is the common property of the people who live in a particular place, and one to which private interests pay deference. The public nature of the image allows the citizens to know that because they share the image, they are citizens of the same place sharing the same way of public life.

Without this or some such picture there is no city. But without particular circumstances, especially those of time and place, and without individuals attempting to build a city in that time and place, there is no picture. Consider these analogies: for a judge to review a case there must be an event that gives rise to a case, but for the thing to be called a case there must be some idea of what relationship a judge might have to the event; for legislators to frame a law there must be something to be done, but for

legislators to be called on to do it requires some expectations about the role of legislators and of legislation; and for an architect to design a building or other part of a city, there must be a function to be satisfied and some idea that can be pictured involving the role of architects and of buildings relative to that function and in the city. In this sense the city, the urban place, is the product of architects' responses to changes over time as each architect interprets the image of the city in a way that is appropriate to the architect's art. The product will be the embodiment in architectural form of the way of public life of those who live in it, for a city from the architect's point of view is first of all the translation into actual form of the way of public life of those who build, change, and maintain it.

III

In the traditional world the architect's image of the city, whether held in the mind or rendered as an actual construction of some part, is limned in one of two broad patterns: one of them a haphazard accumulation, the other a preconceived, finite plan. Actual cities, whether traditional or modernist, turn out to be some mixture of the two, although generally any particular city seems to have more the character of one or the other.

The haphazard is probably the more common. Its origins are in the family (generally tribal in extent) which settles in some place that provides a common core attractive to more families. The settlement grows into a village, and the village might continue to grow beyond what we can reasonably call a village. But no matter how large it becomes, its residents might still think of it as a village, and this way of thinking might be reinforced by the way it is seen, or perhaps only imagined. Thus, its physical character can reveal that no one of importance in it ever pictured the place as more than a village or, at best, as a collection of villages. As in the form so too in the way of life: the village's settled residents are clustered into family groups and only reluc-

Lake Front, Chicago, 1910.

tantly accept alien newcomers; whatever it was that drew the earlier settlers to the place can be satisfied without their help. New non-family members are considered a threat to the good the family offers to its members.

The character and not the size is the essential and distinctive aspect of a village. In both the physical and the social structure, the family unit is the basic unit, even if the settlement stretches across a vast landscape, as in London, where one can picture himself living in a village as easily as he can see himself as a part of a vast city. In America, beached suburbs such as Chicago's Hyde Park or Boston's Dorchester, near-in suburbs such as Evanston or Boston's Brookline, and far-flung satellites like Lake Forest, Illinois or Concord, Massachusetts are as common as isolated outposts in rural districts. In America today we admire such village-like places more than we do the other kind of traditional city, and we think of them as the normative form of American urban settlement. The village seems to offer a picturesque assemblage of small homesteads and their community

facilities and suggest a peacefulness within the resident's soul. These villages seem to defy modernism.

While appearing to be models of the best traditionalism, villages have their deficiencies. We do not look there for the fruits of civilization, the civil fruits whose collective name alone reveal them as the products of the city, unless a city has long before swallowed the village in its core and made those fruits accessible within its parochial bounds. In the great examples of civil achievement the villages of their origins gave way to the cities of their apogee: ancient Athens and Rome, the Florence and Paris which regained a civil character after collapsing into mere villages during the uncivil period of early medieval barbarism, and the leagues of villages that were synthesized to form London and Daniel H. Burnham's Chicago.

The change from village to city or to village within a city involved more than a mere enlargement of population and wealth. It required a realignment of institutional affiliation and loyalty, and that is a very different realignment. To make a city from a

Looking west along Chicago River from an Illinois Central Elevator, 1908.

village requires that the individuals in it accept an idea that does not come easily to a villager, namely, that a person's lot is improved by investing as much of himself outside the family as inside it.

But mere projection is not enough. The extension beyond the family can produce a city only if the investment is in one of the institutions that supplements the family in the moral ordering of the individual's world. Institutions look to the moral well-being of their members and are to be distinguished from arrangements which look merely to getting on with life. Cities are made of institutions, and while there are many kinds of institutions, only a few are capable of making cities. In the traditional world descending to us from classical antiquity, only two have been capable of doing so—the state and the church—and until recently, the state and the church were inseparable. The cities holding these institutions central in their concerns have been hospitable to other institutions, but settlements dedicated primarily to lesser pursuits than those of living justly and well in the state or the church—say, commerce, trade, or manufacturing—have proven inimical to them. The market may make the family wealthy, but only through the church and the good state can it be whole and healthy.

For a village of adequate size to become a city rather than merely a settlement or a large collection of villages requires that it be transformed. That transformation will include a re-imagining of itself and of its parts, but not at the expense of obliterating the identity of the families and villages from which it was formed. The ancient village will be at the core of the modern city.

Cities that do not begin as haphazard accumulations come into being *ex novo*, at once, by following a predetermined picture that includes a set form and finite limit. The picture's design includes a political structure and physical form, but it need not have any people. It can become a city, however, only by drawing to it the number of people required to fulfill the purpose for which it is founded. Those who dwell here consider their personal destinies to be somehow linked to that of the others who find their personal destinies to be somehow linked to that of the others who find their way to it. The family is not necessarily at its core, although the family might be as important to such a place as it is to the city made from the transformation of haphazard settlements.

An *ex novo* city is successful in fulfilling its purpose when the fruits it offers are more enticing than what the village proffers. Experience with our tradition teaches that in this case, as in the one concerning the growth of villages into cities, the fruits will be civil fruits if the aspiration to live in the good state or in the church is the predominate aspiration of the place—predominate, but not necessarily exclusive.

Americans today find more to suspect than to applaud in the most familiar examples of fully-articulated *ex novo* foundations. For example, a distressingly large number misunderstand Plato's *Atlantis* and *Republic* or Thomas More's *Utopia* and consider them examples of fascist authoritarianism obliterating individual liberty, the suppression of the individual in favor of the collective, and the family destroyed in the interest of the state. In like manner, they admire and seek instruction from the formal pattern of a number of places—Alexander the Great's foundations, the Roman colonies and military encampments, the new towns of medieval Europe, the ruling centers for Baroque princes (Karlsruhe; St. Petersburg), cities of would-be saints on Earth (New Haven; Salt Lake City), cities built for profit (Philadelphia, Savannah, Pullman); or cities promulgated as utopian visions of the earthly paradise available through modernism (the visions of Le Corbusier, Walter Gropius, or Frank Lloyd Wright)—but if they knew what the way of life was meant to be in them, they would flee them as Lot's family did Gomorrah. They illustrate the point that no vision of a way of life based on any one person's or one moment's understanding can remain valid for other people later.

Circumstances constantly change. In the life of both the village and the *ex novo* foundation, the modern must invigorate the ancient if a place is to overcome the limitations inevitable in its foundation. In the best examples, the founding ideals remain intact as the place is invested with an expanded civility; while in the less successful, the life of the citizens is debased into the mere pursuit of private gain, however that is measured at the time. Either way, the transformed *ex novo* foundation and the expanded and transformed haphazard village are alike in offering both familial seclusion and its opposite. The village within the fully-fledged city protects the family-centered life of the individual who asks little more of life than what the family offers, while the piazzas and commons facilitate the full maturity of the individual through participation in the city's public life.

IV

In cities, the most important issues are the civil issues. Civil issues involve making choices, they arise only in the city, and they are by nature public. If there is one thing that sets the public life in a city apart from any other way of life, it is the kind of choices it makes available, choices that offer an answer to the question: what good does the individual obtain through living in the city that is not available in any other way of life? Are we dealing with the deficient traditional city Aristotle called a mere league of traders and which St. Augustine epitomized as a den of pirates? Or the equally vacuous modern one that sociology would come to call a relatively large, dense, and permanent settlement of socially heterogeneous individuals and that anthropology would discover as the location of a unique culture? Or is there something better, something that can best be called the classical city as exemplified, at various times, in Plato's *Republic*, More's *Utopia*, Dante's *Paradiso*, Leo Battista Alberti's imaginable city, or the republic Thomas Jefferson sought to bring into being? These cities could not be experienced and then described; they had to be imagined to be described, and the most important thing to imagine about them was the kind of good they offered their citizens. These are classical cities, and to know about them requires setting them apart form all other kinds of cities.

When imagination rather than experience precedes description, the imagination is liberated from the constraints of time and place. While the modernist city must be experienced to be described, the traditional city must be imagined before being described. When the imagined traditional city is sought as a place wherein its citizens can aspire to live lives that are good, just, healthy, and whole, it is a classical city. While imagination precedes description, it does not stand independent of experience. While its origin is in the imagination, the classical city is still a very specific kind of place, one that has a particular purpose and a particular means of achieving it. Its purpose is to be a good city, which it can be insofar as it allows individuals to attempt to act for the good.

Recall the example above of the judge, the legislator, and the architect. In the classical city, the animating picture for the judge is the figure of justice that allows him to discover how justice or injustice is exemplified in any particular act that comes before him. For the legislator it is the composite picture that includes the hopes of the governed to live justly and the restrictions on government that facilitates the protection of the rights people possess by virtue of their being people; he consults this picture each time he exercises the primary art of the legislator, that of prudence, to determine the best relationship between the end that is sought and the means available for reaching it. For the architect it is a formal image of an actual city of buildings, streets, open places, and miscellaneous urban equipment, serving those same ends, and achieving their actual, discrete form each time he or others like him design for a particular site at a specific time and for a concrete function.

In the good city citizens can pursue happiness by practicing the art of living well together. The name of this art is politics, and practicing it requires the proportioning of means to ends. Here the means are the broad range of acts displaying the various special skills that allow the good city to work—the skills of the judge,

legislator, and architect as well as those of the priest, the merchant, the investor and developer and banker, the teacher, the carpenter, and the mason. And here the ends culminate to the greatest extent possible in the best end or purpose of man, which is to live happily, that is, to perfect one's nature and thereby live nobly and well. Such a task requires a classical city and cannot be accomplished with anything else. This is because each person, whether in a classical city or in another kind of city or elsewhere than in a city, does that which he believes is good for himself and assumes responsibility for the choices he makes. No healthy person acts with disregard to self-interest, and every healthy person knows that he cannot live alone and therefore cannot act for himself alone. The city is the arena for the interaction between such individuals, and a classical city is an arena where there is a constant interplay involving the adjustments each citizen makes to balance the demands of the interest in perfecting one's own nature and those of working with others, whether or not they seek the same end for themselves.

This way of thinking about people recognizes that the nature of man does not change, and that because the good city is the city that serves the good in people, its characteristics do not change either. These characteristics are order, proportionality, harmony, prosperity, beauty, elegance—the characteristics, that is, of a place where each citizen lives according to his nature by proportioning his means to the end of living nobly and justly. But because the circumstances within which any two people live differ, the means each one will use to reach the same end will differ. As it is with the citizen, so too must it be with the city, only in larger form. Thus, no two classical cities—no two cities that aspire to be noble and just—can be alike.

And neither can any city or any citizen be perfectly noble and just. If the individual spends a lifetime attempting to know himself only to discover an ever larger ignorance, how much more must this be the case for the city. Because it is the case that without a particular, actual instance, the nature of a thing cannot be known, it follows that the nature of the good city cannot be known

East Lake Shore Drive, Chicago and the Near North Side, c. 1940.

independently of experience of it in some actual place at some particular moment. But this nature cannot be entirely embodied in actual circumstances—in some particular political form, in some unique and fitting social structure, in an urban pattern that accounts for a unique topography, in an architectural appearance arising from the design of particular buildings satisfying well-understood needs called for by the political, social, and urban forms—when that nature is less than perfectly known. Sadly, since we are less than angels, since the greatest gift of our liberty is doubt, nature will always be less than perfectly known, no matter how great the zeal for knowing it and how vast the energies and treasure spent in building the best possible city.

But it is far worse not to expend the zeal and energy. During the lifetime spent attempting to know himself so that he can escape an even larger ignorance, the individual meshes his life with the lives of others, some his contemporaries, others his forebears, and other his predecessor citizens. And so too does the city, which is after all simply the citizen writ large. The history

that an individual writes and a city builds to hold a life that extends into the unknown circumstances of the future is the tale that contains what must be known when proportioning means to ends, that is, of pursuing happiness by living nobly and justly.

V

Another look at the way cities are imagined will amplify the differences between the traditional, the classical, and the modernist city. A traditional city has a clear but vague image of itself, an image that is clear because it is valid for all times but an image that is vague because only the act of picturing it and actually building it in a time and place can give it specificity. The classical city is a particular kind of traditional city. Its image reveals the western tradition's developing understanding of the way the free, skeptical individual citizen may, if he wishes, pursue happiness beyond the family, within the political, public life of the institutions of state (no matter its form: monarchy, oligarchy, democracy, etc.) and church (whether established or disestablished).

The modernist city, on the other hand, is a picture, not an image, a picture that is about its circumstances—this moment, this place, this means, this end, this knowledge, these people— as these take form in the activities that make it work. But work to what end or to produce what? In the modernist city, the work of the judge is interpreting the changing statutes of legislators. The work of the legislator is responding to the changing desires of the electorate and the changing projections of the economic future upon which his fate depends. And the work of the architect is making form from the changing styles of architecture and the changing constraints of economics and technology. In modernism, the city is a convenience at best but never a necessity; these activities in this form can exist whether or not there is a city. The

only commonality between judging, legislating, and designing arises from their being located in something called a city, although the location might be called something else—say, rural countryside, or a "new town in town."

Whatever the locus, it is not imaginable in a general and public way. Lacking is the kind of image allowing a picture based on actual circumstances limning both the city's form and the purpose that form is to serve. Instead of an image or a picture, the modernist city exists in a myriad of very clear, very distinct, and constantly changing pictures with no necessary continuity from one to the next. The latest manner available to the designer producing these pictures uses a computer, which allows him to manipulate the picture to his liking restrained only by the laws of cybernetic technology and unfettered by the ballast of tradition and regard for the laws that allow the life of a community to be a civic life.

The Court of Honor, Chicago's World's Fair, 1893.

The modernist city can, therefore, be whatever each individual wants it to be. How to be a judge, legislator, or architect is spelled out in all sorts of ways that are specific to judges, legislators, and architects but not related to one another as civic activities. Because there is no civic, public connection guiding their activities in a direction that allows each citizen to perfect his nature and thereby to seek his pleasure by living nobly and well, and because there is no image embodying the city's form and its public purpose, an image possessed by all citizens, the modernist city cannot be the classical city. It therefore is the equivalent of the traditional city where trade and piracy are the primary pursuits, unless it follows a different course, say by being a place where the purely modernist values of social perfection or cultural authenticity are sought (even at the expense of the individual), or by dissolving into the traditional village, which at least offers whatever pleasures are available in isolation or in the privacy of the family.

The good, classical city is built by those who know the time and the place in which they are working, and who never lose sight of the role their efforts play in filling out the picture of it that they share with one another. To do this requires coordinating the efforts they exercise on their own behalf with those that others like them undertake for their own sake and for that of the city. And it requires that they share with their fellow citizens a knowledge of what the good city is and of how that city can be built in the circumstances they inhabit.

VI

As an illustration of how some of these ideas can be applied to understanding the history of a particular place, let us take a brief glance at Chicago. Chicago's history is as rich as its architecture. Its architecture makes a rich urban setting. And architectural historians have usually seen its history as an illustration of modernism. Here I will treat it as a classical city.

Meeting of the board of Architects and the Grounds Building Committee of the Columbian Exposition, February 24, 1891.

Chicago began as a trading center and fort, that is, as a traditional village, and then enjoyed a brief life as the *ex nova* foundation of a canal company. It grew too fast to bear the marks of either of these beginnings for very long, although the character laid down by the canal company has remained prominent throughout its history. The city's earliest official, institutional history involved its chartering as a town in 1834. Its incorporation as a municipality in 1837 occurred long before modernism disrupted traditionalism in America, although the forces of trade, commerce, and manufacturing that would support modernism quickly tapped into the riches available through the traffic nourishing Chicago. When its second half-century as an incorporated entity began, it appeared that the city poised between the lake and the prairie would become a mere dreary appendage of the European workshops that Jefferson had said threatened the liberty of the American polity, until the city suddenly refashioned itself as a classical city. For more than three decades spanning the turn of the century, it retained that character until its canal company origins and the forces at work in the larger world overwhelmed it and transformed it into the desolate modernist city it has become today.

The transforming event in the coarse workshop city's history was its hosting of the World's Columbian Exposition of 1893, an event that was so profound, as its unpredicted aftermath revealed, that it served as the city's virtual re-founding. The energies devoted to its transformation extended over a period beginning with the Fair's planning and execution, crystallizing in the publication in 1909 of Daniel H. Burnham and Edward Bennett's *Plan of Chicago*, and extending for nearly another two decades until the energy was spent and the spirit of transformation atrophied. The timing was fortunate, for that was perhaps the most recent moment such a re-founding might have been possible, a moment when traditional ideas honed by classical knowledge could still permeate the thought of those who were vested with the authority to undertake great things, a moment when the modern still acted as a commentary on the ancient, the moment, that is, just before those with better, more up-to-date modernist ideas took charge.

We miss seeing traditionalist, classical Chicago in the *Plan* when we follow modernist historians in seeing the Plan's pictures as a literal presentation of what was intended for Chicago's physical form. A proper interpretation requires a more subtle reading of the picture to find the image it fleshes out. This calls for recognizing its hierarchical differentiation between that which is important because it facilitates and that which is important because it deserves facilitation. In the first category were things justified as means to an end. The material in this category concentrated on Chicago as an efficient industrial, commercial, and transportation nexus. Here the material is presented as a much more literal diagram or design than the other category, that which is justified as an end that is good in itself. The presentation of this material is less literal and more an image or a sketch. The image

Group of World's Fair Architects, Artists, and Officials, May, 1891.

of the new city hall, for example, was presented more to remind Chicagoans of Richard Morris Hunt's Administration Building at the Fair, the administrative center for the most recent model of the renewed Chicago, than to suggest what their brand new city hall should have looked like, just as its siting was more a picture of where the city's center of gravity was or would be than a proposal for land acquisition and street rebuilding. A new city hall with a very different form on a very different site was under construction even as the *Plan* was being prepared, so there was never the slightest thought that a new city hall would soon be built according to the suggestions of the *Plan*.

Because its more important parts were seen and presented more as an image than as diagrams or as a sketch than as designs, the *Plan* was able to remain the persuasive image of Chicago for decades. This was the city where men would work to grow in both prosperity and civility and where they might live nobly and justly by understanding the relationship between ends and means and the hierarchical relationship between the several desires a city makes available to people.

To build the city presented in the *Plan* required a series of actions by official bodies and independent individuals, all of whom adhered to its general lineaments while filling in the piece that fell under some particular purview. This was easier to do than we might imagine today because the people who set about to build the *Plan*'s city were willing to follow a few general rules that since then have fallen into desuetude and largely passed from memory. They are the rules that have been followed whenever those practicing the art of architecture have set about to build a Beautiful and Decorous City to hold the Good City, that is, ever since conscious urban design became possible during the Renaissance.[2]

These rules follow from certain premises. One premise is that the functions buildings serve are established by the larger civic purposes the city attempts to reach. Thus, for example, one civic purpose is that people live nobly and justly. This calls for a wide range of specific functions that require public buildings

housing the institutions of the state ranging from courthouses and city halls on down through schools to fire houses and even animal pounds, prisons, and pumping plants. Another civic purpose is that people reside in safety and comfort, indeed in the safety and comfort of the family, a purpose served by domestic structures both private and public (e.g., hospitals and boarding schools). And another is that they be able to sustain themselves, which in a city requires industrial and commercial structures whose function is to produce wealth, to make available the means of sustaining life, and to enjoy the fruits of prosperity.

One rule that follows from this is that the composition of the city's image must control the appearance of its embodiment in an actual picture or place so that the formal composition can convey the relative importance of the parts in achieving these ends. Thus, for example, when circumstances allow, the most important buildings and places should be central, free-standing, and larger. This rule concerning location and composition is supplemented by another, more complicated rule. It is based on the idea that there is a limited number of ideal building types, each of which accommodates one of the few fundamental activities comprising all that is essential in pursuing the good life within the civil realm. Corresponding to them is a limited range of designs for the various functional types of buildings—for example, residential buildings or commercial and industrial buildings—each with a limited range of distinct compositional patterns established by the practice of a place. Using them allows a building's role among the purposes of the city to be identified.

Traditional architecture has always followed these and a few other, cognate rules. Within traditional design, the variety of ever-modern classical architecture provides the best evidence of the liberty they provide. That they need not lead to uniformity, sterility, and banality is clear, since even lowly industrial buildings lend themselves to a great deal of variety without disguising themselves as something they are not or confusing the representation of their role in the city. That identity is important, for, in the classical city, just as being a merchant is different from being

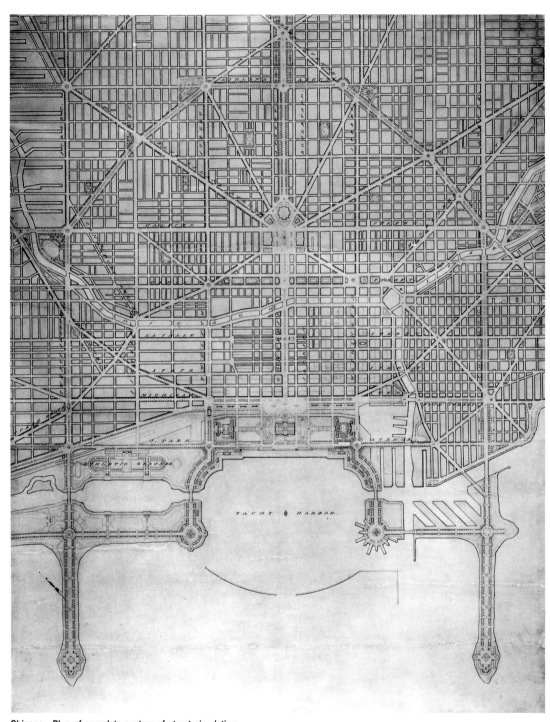

Chicago. Plan of complete system of street circulation.

The Chicago Plan exhibited at Dusseldorf, August 1910.

a judge, so too among buildings no one should mistake a place devoted to industry for a public building or dwelling. (Note that in the present confusion about such matters, buildings built for industry and representing themselves as such have been converted to public and residential uses.)

Another rule is based on the premise that within each range of functional building types, the status of particular examples differs according to how central they are in serving the most important things in a city. In a league of traders or band of pirates seeking wealth alone, the buildings best able to generate or maintain wealth will be the most central, and will appear to be so. Currently and with increasing clarity, Chicago's Loop and upper Michigan Avenue illustrate this. The form of a city whose social and political structure is based on the lessons of natural science hitched to the idea of progress can be exemplified by the 1889 Exposition in Paris, where the central axis drew together the two great examples of what the practical application of natural science could accomplish. At one end was Ferdinand Dutert's cavernous

Galerie des Machines filled with its marvels of applied science; at the other rose Gustave Eiffel's lofty Tower offering a vertiginous viewpoint to those on it and an inspiring vision of an achieved aspiration to others.

Compositional patterns do not carry any particular content. The one used in 1889 was also used for the Chicago fair where the axis ran from the old world (Columbus on the triumphal arch at the lake's edge) through the statue of the Republic and fountain of prosperity to its culmination in the Administration Building. Here society is not to be perfected as if it is a machine or built up as if a tower. Instead, the governments of the new world become the means of promoting the fruits of the earth, of the fields, and of the industry and ingenuity of men, fruits that were laid out for display within the buildings flanking the great central basin where they could support and sustain the most important thing, the administration of those things for the good and prosperity of people. That picture of the Fair was an embodiment of an image, and it was that image that was used to picture Chicago in 1909.

We can see the new, transformed, refounded classical Chicago by looking at the pictures Chicagoans made from the image emerging from the refounding. Some of them are in the Plan, but more concrete examples of them are in the buildings the next generation of Chicagoans built to embody the image and implement the Plan. To see the pictures clearly requires using another rule for building, which says that the relative importance or status of a building is indicated by the relative level of finish given the design and the quality of the materials and workmanship used in its construction. This dual aspect of finish, when taken in conjunction with the pattern used to represent a building's functional type, completes the most important determinants for the design of buildings in a classical city.

A different but not unimportant issue in interpreting the picture's embodiment of Chicago's newly discovered image is that of a building's style. At the time the Plan was formulated, the style of the various buildings used to make the image of the Plan concrete was a great preoccupation of architects. The style chosen—that of the currently modern form of ancient classical architecture—connected the Plan with the nation's roots in ancient classical thought and in its own founding when the then-currently modern forms of ancient classical architecture were used for the buildings and cities erected as repositories of the new birth of freedom. But the choice of the classical did not exclude other choices. Instead, for an age immersed in what Geoffrey Scott, the apologist for what might be called an architecture of kinaesthetic formalism, would condemn as the Romantic Fallacy, choosing one rather than another historical style was less a formal choice than one based on using the style to refer to suggestions about how the building fitted into a larger framework of civil life. The choice supplemented the suggestions conveyed by following the rules to provide further clarity about both the specific function and its relative place within the hierarchical scheme of things by furnishing certain conventional associative values. For example, in general, classical referred to the larger, urban and civil public ideas of a place while the Gothic suggested the village-scale importance of family and village-neighborhood or suburban township. Both styles provided ample opportunity for small-scale details in the form of various design motifs or recognizable collections of architectural elements, inscriptions, and so on. The role of these finishing touches, however, was always established by the larger aspects of design, namely, compositional pattern and level of finish.

The published *Plan of Chicago* is only the most easily accessible picture of the image guiding the generation of architects who followed the rules embedded in the image as they built in the transformed Chicago, a generation that included Holabird and Roche, Daniel H. Burnham and the successor firms including Graham, Anderson, Probst, and White, as well as others who are less well known such as Benjamin Marshall and Alfred Alschuler. In their work there is seldom any ambiguity about the purpose, function, or status of a building, unless that ambiguity is built into the design or the design is meant to challenge the place others might have assigned such a building. One must, of course, be alert to the intrusion of outside circumstances that prevented the construction of the best possible embodiment of the image (one thinks for example of the political manipulations, greed, and self-seeking vainglory of the principals involved in reducing the *Plan*'s proposed package freight terminal at the mouth of the Chicago River into Navy Pier). And it is a fact that in any moment, not all architects and clients are equally clear-sighted and able. Think, for example, of what the city would have looked like if some of the local architects who submitted entries to the 1922 *Chicago Tribune* competition had been given commissions for large, conspicuous buildings. Architects such as Benjamin Olson, Paul Gerhardt, and C.A. Eckstorm were excellent designers of three-story flat buildings and of industrial and commercial loft buildings, and it is a blessing that they stuck to their specialties.

The city Chicagoans built is the product of talent properly applied to projects worth doing within a larger scheme of things. To a greater extent than had been the case in the pre-transformed

Chicago and in the Chicago of the next generation, what they produced was remarkable because architects, clients, and public officials shared a civil, architectural, and urban image. The admirable place they built is the result of their willingness to be guided by that image rather than the result of the stylistic, social, economic, technological, demographic, and other forces commonly used to explain the history of Chicago architecture. In the good civic design they pursued, each building fits into the general design patterns that others were using as they together built the Beautiful and Decorous City. It is not their self-expression we are to admire, but their skillful manipulation of a set of propositions they shared with one another and their predecessors back through the tradition of classical city building.

That Chicago no longer exists. The chain of tradition was broken—a chain that, some would say, worked for the good by tying classical Chicago to its illustrious predecessors, making it like them, and thereby allowing for its comparison with them, a chain that, as others would say, bound the city's architects and other residents to a debilitating prison of tradition and precedent preventing the liberation of their individuality. Are we, when looking at a Chicago from that era, to see it as a part of a larger image or as a beacon pointing to a future that promises more than the past delivered and makes all in the past obsolete? Did the Fair re-found Chicago, or did it confound it with such confusion that, as Louis Sullivan said, "The damage wrought by the [Chicago] World's Fair [of 1893] will last for half a century from its date, if not longer."[3] By the time that half-century had elapsed, architects had managed to put the Fair behind them, and ever since, Chicago architecture has always been changing, the newest perforce being the best, and Sullivan serving as the titular saint of Chicago architecture. But suppose instead it had been Burnham?

NOTES

1 For this point see, *inter alia*, Robert Jan van Pelt in van Pelt and C.W. Westfall, *Architectural Principles in the Age of Historicism* (New Haven and London: Yale University Press, 1991), chapter 1; and Bernard Knox, "The Oldest Dead White European Males," in *The Oldest Dead White European Males and Other Reflections on the Classics* (New York and London: W.W. Norton, 1993).

2 The following material draws on these earlier studies: "Chicago's Better Tall Apartment Buildings: 1871-1923," *Architectura*, XXI (2/1991),177-208; "The Classical City, Chicago, and Alfred S. Alschuler," *Threshold: Journal of the School of Architecture, University of Illinois at Chicago*, (5/6, 1991), 90-102 (published in a way which distorts my thought because the first half which includes the argument presented here was excised without my approval); "From Homes to Towers: A Century of Chicago's Best Hotels and Tall Apartment Buildings," *Chicago Architecture 1872-1922: Birth of a Metropolis*, ed. John Zukowsky, (Munich: Prestel-Verlang and The Art Institute of Chicago, 1987), 267-289; "Buildings Serving Commerce", *Chicago Architecture 1872-1922*, 77-89; "Home at the Top: Domesticating Chicago's Tall Apartment Buildings," *Chicago History*, XIV (1985), 20-39; "Benjamin Howard Marshall of Chicago," *The Chicago Architectural Journal*, II (1982), pp.8-27;

"The Golden Age of Chicago Apartments," *Inland Architect*, XXIV, no. 9 (1980), 18-26; "Manners Matter," *Inland Architect*, XXIV, no. 3 (1980), 19-23. For a general treatment of the approach taken here see my chapters in *Architectural Principles in the Age of Historicism*.

3 Louis H. Sullivan, *The Autobiography of an Idea*, (New York: 1956, original ed., 1924), 325.

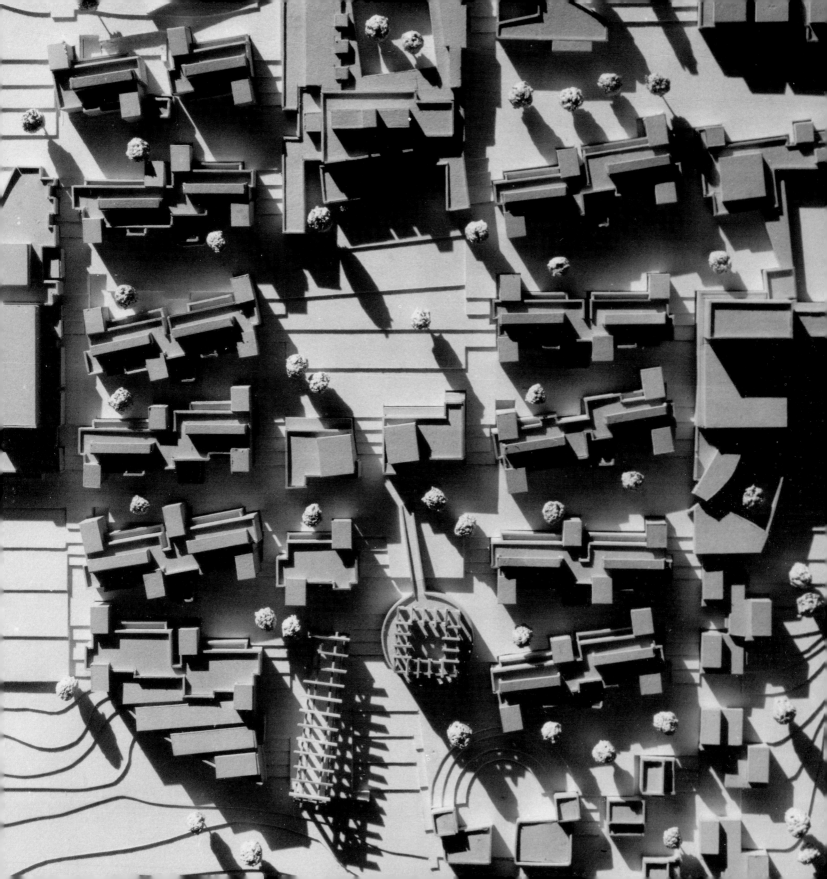

A NATIVE AMERICAN PREPARATORY SCHOOL

DONALD B. GENASCI
OMID MIRARABSHAHI

Donald B. Genasci is a Professor of Architecture at the University of Oregon and is Principal of the firm Donald B. Genasci and Associates, based in Portland.

Omid Mirarabshahi is an Associate Partner in the firm Donald B. Genasci and Associates.

Aerial view of Site Model. Native American Preparatory School.

The Pecos Valley of New Mexico provides the setting for the following proposal for a Preparatory School for Native Americans. Bounded on the north by a dramatic 300-foot-high rimrock stretching nearly 300 miles, and accessed by nearby Interstate 25, the School's context is at once ancient and modern. In programmatic terms, the school's mission is to provide an educational facility where the brightest Native American students from the surrounding regions can gather and live within a unique learning environment. To satisfy this aim, our design of the School attempts to integrate requirements for learning with the ideal of communal dwelling. Living facilities for students and faculty are placed alongside the educational and communal buildings which constitute the heart of the institution: Classrooms, Auditorium, Music Building, Gymnasium, Library, Student Center, Amphitheater and a Spiritual Focus Building.

At every level of the design we sought to reinforce the concept of the School as a village. While our proposal focuses on the School as a cohesive community of students and teachers, we thought it equally important that it reflect the several cultures and histories of its diverse student body. These histories and traditions are recollected architecturally through references to a number of ancient and traditional Native American settlements. Rather than merely repeat the pattern and forms of any one known settlement, elements from several settlements are abstracted and combined in a way that might better address the diverse cultural heritage of the School. Further, the precise application of these forms attempts to develop a dialogue between physical form, ritual, and daily life.

Historically, dwellings in Native American villages are built in groups; they are rarely sited as individual buildings. This emphasis on the collective is taken up in the design of the School through the strategy of clustering. This can be seen most clearly in the organization

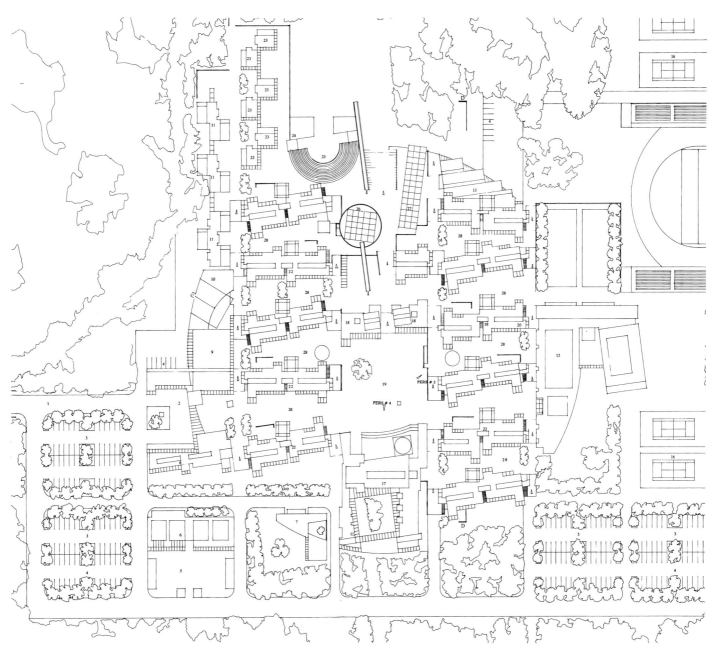

Site Plan.

Index of program spaces: 1-Entry Drive 2-Entry Drop-off 3-Parking 4-Staff Parking 5-Maintenance Yard 6-Maintenance Facility 7-Headmaster's Residence 8-Administration 9-Auditorium 10-Music Building 11-Fine Arts 12-Gymnasium 13-Dining Hall 14-Playing Fields 15-Running Track 16-Tennis Courts 17-Library/Resource Center 18-Student Center 19-Main Square 20-Laundry 21-Lounge 22-Classroom/Dormitory 23-Visiting Artists Residence 24-Theater Stage 25-Amphitheater 26-Spiritual Focus Building 27-Rain House 28-Dormitory Courtyards

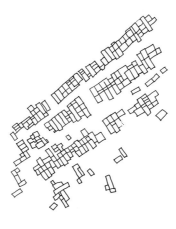

Plans of three historic pueblos. Penasco Blanco, Acoma, and Sichomovi.

of the classrooms and living units about small courtyards, and in the loose assembly of public and ceremonial buildings fronting a public square. In part, the clustering arrangement was chosen for its association with historic villages of the Southwest, particularly those of the neighboring Anasazi and Pecos pueblos. In addition, clustered arrangements serve as the basis for a social order oriented to the collective, and collective living. Another dominant theme carried through various levels of the design is the symbolic inscription of the circle. Recalling the plan of Penasco Blanco, a large circle marks the perimeter of the school, suggesting both protection and social unity. At a smaller scale, the circle is used as a generating figure for ceremonial buildings and spaces throughout the plan. Such notions as unity, emergence (from the underworld), and education are a few of the many mythological and iconographic associations of the circle found in tribes across the North American continent.

Hierarchies of public space within the school were developed using a range of traditional spatial types. These include the main square, the wide street, domestic courtyards, and the semi-private realms of covered porches. The main public square is a chief organizing element of the plan. Major shared spaces and public buildings are placed adjacent to the main square to foster casual social interaction and to accommodate the ceremonial and ritual events associated with them. A primary east-west street crosses the southern edge of the square, anchored by an Entry Court on one end, and the Gymnasium on the other. This street serves as a mediating zone between the Students Center and the Spiritual Focus Building to the north, and the Library/Resource Center to the south.

Wide streets running north and south ramp up the site to connect each of the School's five terraces and a system of smaller residential courtyards. The north-south streets also establish

View of Library/Resource Center.

visual links to the surrounding landscape of the Pecos Valley, while smaller streets and courtyards are generally terminated by larger buildings at the perimeter. Living accommodations for students and faculty are situated above the classrooms and the student center. Organized around long courtyards, the residences are fronted by porches extending the length of the building to encourage casual interaction with people in the street.

Landscaping throughout the School uses native plant species of the New Mexico region, which were placed in the manner of historic villages. Existing stands of conifers and several small-leafed cottonwoods found on the site were also incorporated into the plan. Following Anasazi custom, one large symbolic tree is placed in the central square near the Library/Resource Center. In a very practical way, indigenous plants provide a vital resource for both the enactment of tribal rituals and the practice of traditional medicine.

Indigenous building materials and construction methods were employed throughout the School. Public buildings, such as

the Spiritual Focus Building, as well as retaining walls and courtyard structures are constructed of traditional adobe. Less public structures are built of stucco over concrete block or wood frame. Additionally, wood-framed trellises are used extensively in public and private areas to shade windows and pedestrians from the summer sun. Traditional construction methods were proposed as part of a continuing program to teach native crafts and building techniques.

The Native American Preparatory School, like any village community, will succeed only if it fosters the social and intellectual welfare of its residents. While the proposed design of the School pays homage to the social and symbolic heritage of traditional village forms, elements were chosen that also represent ideals relevant to modern Native American society. We firmly believe that only through a continuing dialogue between traditional ideas and contemporary facts can students begin a critical and thoughtful understanding of the modern world. The design for the School does not rely on historical quotation, nor

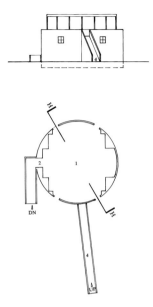

Spiritual Focus Building. Elevation and Plan.

does it abandon traditional forms in the name of cultural neutrality. Instead we have attempted to abstract traditional forms in ways that address contemporary relationships. Our design for the Native American Preparatory School seeks to use the elements of traditional architecture to go beyond function, and to develop a symbolic architecture engaged in a vital dialogue between historical and contemporary ideas.

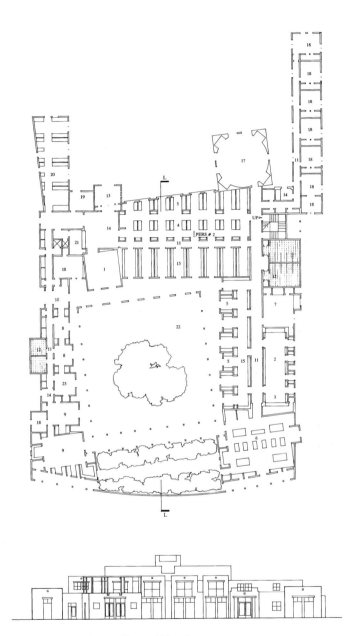

Library/Resource Center. Plan and Elevation.

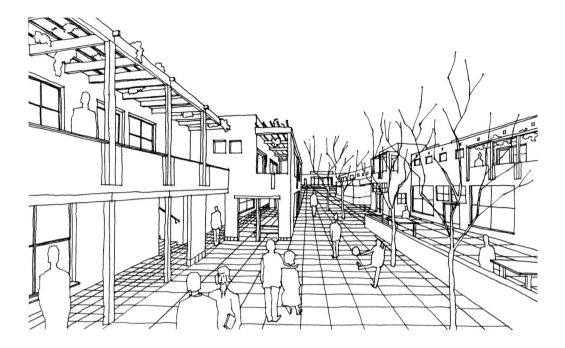

View of residential courtyard.

View of Classroom Building.

**Typical Classroom/Dormitory Building.
Courtyard Elevation, Second Floor
Plan, and First Floor Plan.**

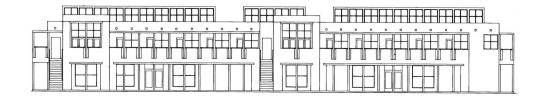

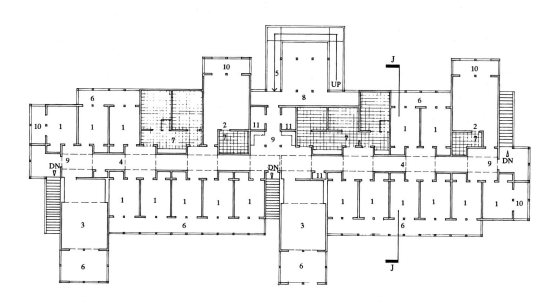

PROJECT CREDITS

"A Native American Preparatory School,"
Santa Fe, New Mexico (1992): Partner-
in-Charge, Donald B. Genasci; Project
Designer, Omid Mirarabshahi;
Production, Mat Sykes and Jim Dixon.

All images courtesy of the author.

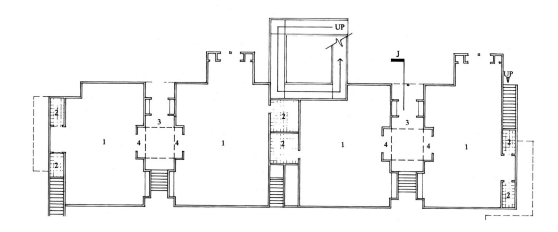

CIVITAS LOST

BRIAN KELLY

Brian Kelly is Associate Professor of Architecture at the University of Maryland at College Park.

What man loses by the social contract is his natural liberty and the absolute right to anything that tempts him and that he can take; what he gains by the social contract is civil liberty and the right of property in what he possesses. ...We might also add that man acquires with civil society, moral freedom, which alone makes man the master of himself; for to be governed by appetite alone is slavery, while obedience to a law one prescribes to one self is freedom.

Jean Jacques Rousseau, *The Social Contract* [1]

The need for rules is a point of difficulty for those who, wrongly equating Intellect with intelligence, balk at the mere mention of forms and constraints — fetters, as they think, on the 'free mind' for whose sake they are quick to feel indignant, while they associate everything dull and retrograde with the word 'convention.' Here ... the alphabet is suggestive: it is a device of limitless and therefore 'free' application. You can combine its elements in millions of ways to refer to an infinity of things in hundreds of tongues, including the mathematical. But its order and its shapes are rigid. You cannot look up the simplest word in a dictionary, you cannot find your friend's telephone number, unless you know the letters in their arbitrary forms and conventional order.

Jacques Barzun, *The House of Intellect* [2]

Many interpretations of modern architecture have been predicated on the notion that the abandonment of the Five Orders and all that they represented rendered architecture free of the determinist/historicist bonds of the past. Freed from the tyranny of style, preconception, and tradition, the modern architect was supposed to revel in a new found state of innocence

Laugier's Primitive Hut.

analogous to that of primitive man. With these complexities and formalities removed it was postulated that solutions to even the most pressing problems were to be found waiting patiently around the corner.

As David Watkin pointed out in *Morality and Architecture*, much of the rhetoric upon which modern architects based pleas for their revolution against tradition were founded upon assumptions of historical and technological determinism, notions of cultural progress, and the Zeitgeist. Watkin says:

> Architectural historians have...found it easy to fall back on the belief in a unitary, all-pervasive Zeitgeist. One important reason for this is that modern art history began in the nineteenth century as a by-product of history and the philosophy of culture in Germany; the rapid growth of popular Marxist sociology, which has a similar intellectual origin, has also played an influential role. Thus everything is seen as a 'reflection' of something else —the economic structure, the spirit of the age, the prevailing theology, and so on. There is also an evolutionary assumption that in each epoch a new economic structure or a new Zeitgeist is 'struggling to be born.' It thus becomes the obligation of the creative spirits, be they poets, architects, or whatever, to 'express' the new nascent spirit. To express an antiquated Zeitgeist is to be condemned as a poor artist or architect. [3]

This conception of history can be attributed to the influence of Hegelian philosophy upon the founders of the disciplines of art and cultural history. The Hegelian concept of history can be seen as an adaptation of theological principles for secular philosophical purposes. Ernst Gombrich in his essay, "In Search of Cultural History," notes that "the history of the universe was for Hegel the history of God creating Himself and the history of mankind was in the same sense the continuous Incarnation of the Spirit."[4] Gombrich continues his interpretation of Hegel by suggesting that the philosopher presents "an extension, or possibly a perversion of the Christian interpretation of providential history."[5] Hegel substitutes the Zeitgeist for the Divine Architect who orchestrates the actions of people and nations. This idea devalues the role of individual contribution to the forces of history by favoring a collective will.

The collective will is, in Hegelian terms, defined by a common center shared by religion, constitution, morality, law, customs, science, art, and technology.[6] If a Hegelian historian were to examine, for example, the history of law of a given people at a given time and were he to be true to his course of pursuit, he would find that the history of law maintained the same origins as the history of art as well as those of religion, constitution, and morality. Gombrich is critical of this notion of history, for it masks the influence of preconceived ideas upon an examination of the past. For the historian to remain true to his course, he must have a priori knowledge to impose upon the pursuit of history. Gombrich says:

> Hegel admits that you can only practice this art when you are familiar with the *a priori* knowledge deduced from his system, but he claims that the same is true of astronomers like Kepler, who must be familiar with the *a priori* laws of geometry to discover the cosmic laws of motion. The comparison is clearly misleading and I should like to replace it by another. Hegel's historian practices exegetics. His *a priori* knowledge is less like that of an astronomer than like that of a devout interpreter of the Scriptures who knows, for instance, that every event described in the Old Testament can be interpreted as foreshadowing another event described in the Gospels. The Jews crossing the Red Sea are a type for the anti-type of Christ's Baptism, Melchisedek offering Abraham bread and wine signifies the Eucharist. For God did not only reveal His plan through the mouth of the prophets, but also in ordering the events themselves.[7]

Gombrich gives credit to Jacob Burkhardt for inadvertently introducing Hegelian methodology to the study of the history of art. Gombrich illustrates his claim with a quote from a letter written by Burkhardt to a friend seeking advice upon writing on the arts: "Conceive your task as follows: How does the spirit of the fifteenth century express itself in painting? Then everything becomes simple."[8] Burkhardt suggests that his friend follow the course of establishing a preconceived notion about the history of a particular time and then assemble an interpretation of events to substantiate the bias.[9] Historical conclusions when derived according to this method become self-fulfilling prophecies; tautologies based upon the original hypothesis.

A similar criticism might be levied against historians who practice historical materialism: Marxism. In his book, *The Italian Renaissance Culture and Society in Italy*, Peter Burke suggests that approaches based upon either "the history of the spirit" or a history based upon social/economic criteria present problems. Having offered initial criticism on the topic of *Geistesgeschichte*, with particular attention to work of Burkhardt, Burke directs his examination to include Marxist methodology:

> ...'the history of spirit' ...begin[s] with ideas rather than with everyday life, stress consensus at the expense of cultural and social conflict and assume somewhat vague connections between different activities. Historical materialists, on the other hand, start with their feet on the earth of everyday life and move upwards to ideas, stress conflict at the expense of consensus and tend to assume that culture, which is an expression of 'ideology', is determined—directly or indirectly—by economic and social 'base.'[10]

While Hegelian ideology might cause the historian to become absorbed with the pursuit of ideas at the expense of actual social constructs, the follower of a Marxist ideology might in a similar manner concentrate upon the social and economic particulars while missing common ideologies. In the end, unstated preconceptions potentially affect the interpretation of historical events.[11]

Karl Popper suggested in his book, *The Poverty of Historicism*, that it was impossible to write history, no less to conduct one's daily activities without preconceptions. Popper says that "the only way out of this difficulty is, I believe, consciously to introduce a *preconceived selective point of view* into one's history...this does not mean that we may twist the facts until they fit the framework of preconceived ideas, or that we may neglect the facts that do not fit."[12] Watkin's criticism of architectural history, as well, centers on the notion that historians who endorse the Hegelian method are unaware that they examine their subject through a filter of preconceived ideas and that these ideas influence the formulation of conclusions. Watkin cites theorists and historians from Pugin to Giedion for practicing this form of historiography. Sir Nikolaus Pevsner is accorded dubious honors by Watkin. He is deemed the most notorious of the recent historians because he utilized Hegelian methodology in interpreting history, but he also proceeded to endorse and manipulate particular contemporary movements because they fit his *a priori* criteria.[13]

The Zeitgeist is supposed, in Hegelian terms, to be a spontaneous expression of the collective will. Because personalities are seen to be subordinate to the collective will, individuals do not create the Zeitgeist, rather the opposite; it reveals itself by speaking through particular characters. The more articulate the individual's annunciation of the "spirit" the more apt he or she is to be deemed genius. Personalities who do not articulate the Zeitgeist, who do not adhere to what has been deemed to be the collective will are either as in the case of Michelangelo, characters who have risen above their age, or as Watkin notes is the case with Pevsner's treatment of Lutyens, presumed to be out of step with the times.[14]

One model that has been proposed to describe the Zeitgeist likens the phenomena to the parlor game of Ouija. There exist two prevalent beliefs, the first being that the pointer is moved by some fantastical and mystical spiritual force that is channeled through the collective subconscious of the participants. This is the position that the believer in the occult would maintain. Then there is the explanation that the game is actually the product of two types of players; the pushers and the pushed. Even in the second scenario the players may be unaware of incremental effects of numerous nervous twitches or minute muscle spasms. In both scenarios the pointer moves, but the critical difference is in the explanation of the cause. The generalizable lesson may be stated: although the Zeitgeist in some cases may constitute an independent expression of the collective will, it is equally possible and more probable that the phenomena of the Zeitgeist is the product of cumulative actions of individuals and personalities who either overtly seek to create a particular cultural phenomena or do so inadvertently.

Watkin also relates notions of technological determinism to expressions of the Zeitgeist.[15] He says that "the belief in the absolute value of adhering to the requirements of technology derives in part from a belief in the spirit of the age and that the spirit has come to reside in the machine."[16] Both Watkin and Popper suggest that "such a preoccupation leads to a belief in the urgency of novelty and change."[17] This position connects the Zeitgeist with notions of stylistic change that fuel a continuous frenzy of invention. Since it is the obligation of each artist to express the Zeitgeist, lest he or she desire to be left behind in the wake of progress, artist, poet, musician, theologian, and architect will have to abandon the styles of the previous generation in order to facilitate the expression of the present Zeitgeist. No sooner will their creations be complete than the next generation will enter the picture to ensure the obsolescence of the previous generation's efforts. Consequently, the ever present need to change styles arises in order not to be associated with the generations of the past. *Style*, that word so deplored in modern architectural literature, becomes simultaneously the central focus of both attack and invention for those attempting to express the spirit of the age. In this process it is easy to see how "the new"

and "the inventive" receive a positive reception while, "tradition" and "convention" are immediately cast in a negative role. In American culture, possibly like nowhere else, *new* is often synonymous with improved, virtuous, or better. The inventors of the last 100 years—Bell, Edison, and Ford—are often heralded as the gods of American culture and commerce. But the substitution of one Zeitgeist for another is presumably not motivated by such complex value judgments. It is, we are told, a spontaneous expression of the collective will! As a result, the cannibalization of styles or progress, going beyond that of the current style, becomes an absurd objective of the artist.

Clearly, progress in artistic or cultural terms is problematic since the Zeitgeist is only concerned with change as a representation of the collective will, change for its own sake, and not change as reflective of a value judgment: change for the better or for the worse. Were we to subscribe to a notion of progress in the arts, Giotto would naturally be seen as superior to Cimabue, for did he not refine the human figure? Giotto, however, would yield to Leonardo since the latter made scientific anatomical studies. Leonardo in turn would presumably fall to Michelangelo, who had perfected *contrapposto*. Presumably, this fatuous line of succession could be carried through to present time. While the illustration above readily, and possibly somewhat reductively, points out the problem with notions of progress when applied to art history, a no less hierarchical yet possibly less linear view of history has often infiltrated the classroom. It wasn't all that long ago that Baroque architecture was taught as a degenerate form of the Renaissance, while inventive Greek architecture was often presented as superior to the imitative architecture of the Romans, and Neo-classical architecture was deemed rightly superior to the Renaissance on the basis of archaeological accuracy.

The flawed notion of progress in art forms a basis for T.S. Eliot's essay, "Tradition and the Individual Talent." Eliot was writing to an audience of potential poets, but we can see that the advice could readily be directed to architects, artists and historians as well: "He [the poet] must be quite aware of the obvious fact that art never improves, but that the material of art is never quite the same."[18]

Through a rejection of progress, Eliot's poet, now aware that art never improves, is bound to discover value in the undertaking of a critical examination of the traditions of his or her discipline. However, Eliot's point is clear: though art may not be subject to progress, it is not the role of the poet merely to repeat the efforts of the past. Eliot's poet is thrust into a situation in which he or she must develop a critical posture toward tradition. The poet must analyze, evaluate, consider, and weigh the often conflicting attributes of the artistic tradition in relation to the present predicament. Eliot writes, "...if the only form of tradition, of handing down consisted in following the ways of the immediate generation before us in a blind or timid adherence to its successes, 'tradition' should possibly be discouraged."[19]

Eliot does not believe that the method of associating oneself with tradition is so inflexibly defined as to cause subsequent generations to practice a form of discipleship. For Eliot, tradition is not a one-way street. It is not merely passed along unaffected or unaltered from one generation to the next. Eliot's notion of tradition is interactive and is far from being determinist:

> Tradition is a matter of wider significance. It cannot be inherited, and if you want it you must obtain it by great labor. It involves, in the first place, the historical sense, which we may call nearly indispensable to anyone who would continue to be a poet beyond his twenty-fifth year...This historical sense, which is a sense of timelessness as well as of the temporal and of the timelessness and of the temporal together, is what makes a writer traditional. And it is at the same time what makes a writer most acutely conscious of his place in time, of his own contemporaneity...No poet, no artist of any art, has his complete meaning alone.[20]

Another scholar, Jaroslav Pelikan presents a particularly stimulating examination of tradition in his book, *The Vindication of Tradition*. Pelikan defines *tradition* as distinct from *traditionalism*. "Tradition," he writes, "is the living faith of the dead, traditionalism is the dead faith of the living."[21] Pelikan contends that we often tend to confuse the positive qualities of tradition with the more suspect characteristics of traditionalism:

> The reformers of every age, whether political or religious or literary, have protested against the tyranny of the dead, and doing so they have called for innovation and insight in place of tradition.[22]

Pelikan places tradition in direct opposition to the notion of insight, which sponsors innovation, transformation, and deviation from precedent. He notes that "the recognition of the tension between tradition and insight is itself an ineradicable element of the tradition itself, which must therefore not be identified with traditionalism that seeks to preserve it by embalming it."[23] The author demonstrates that insight itself derives from a profound understanding of tradition. For Pelikan, the rediscovery of tradition and the development of insight comes through repetition, a ritualistic recitation of conventions and customs:

> The condescending attitude that many interpreters toward such recitation, which often includes a stated preference for what is called 'understanding,' fails to recognize that during most of intellectual history understanding has come through reciting, or, to recur to the Emersonian antimony, that insight was achieved by means of tradition.[24]

Pelikan maintains that in order to understand our present predicament we must take the time to evaluate the role of tradition in regard to contemporary society. He suggests that tradition and departure from traditions have played an important role in the conception of modern life. Pelikan also writes that a distinction should be made between the rediscovery of tradition and its recovery; that through a rediscovery of tradition one can intuit the "first principles" from which successive generations of custom developed, transformed, and mutated. Simply to seek to recover tradition, a more fundamentalist action, does not imply the scrutiny of tradition by the forces of insight; nor does it suggest a dialectical, and in Pelikan's opinion preferred, relationship between the present and the past. He writes, "...the history of... tradition is also the history of the critical re-examination of the tradition that has been made obligatory not by the inner dynamic of the tradition itself, but by outsiders who have raised questions about the unexamined assumptions in the tradition."[25]

Both Eliot and Pelikan understand tradition not as a force of absolute authority but rather as an interactive, discursive, and dialectical entity that is revealed through study, comparison, analysis, and ultimately selection or judgment. For Eliot, the judgment of a poet's efforts cannot be seen as a process that responds solely to the internally referential characteristics of the artist. Judgment for Eliot is an evaluation of the relationship between the artist and his or her intellectual tradition:

> In a peculiar sense he [the poet] will be aware also that he must inevitably be judged by the standards of the past. I say judged, not amputated, by them; not judged to be as good as, or worse or better than, the dead; and certainly not judged by the canons of dead critics. It is a judgment, a comparison, in which two things are measured by each other.[26]

In Eliot's analysis, the major burden of proof of a poet's merit lies with the artist as opposed to the tradition. While the individual artist may indeed play a substantive role in the modification of the tradition, Eliot clearly states that a hierarchy exists in the relationship between an artist and the body of knowledge of which the tradition is comprised:

He [the poet] must be aware that the mind of

Europe—the mind of his own country—a mind which he learns in time to be much more important than his own private mind—is a mind which changes, and that this change is a development which abandons nothing en route, which does not superannuate Shakespeare, or Homer, or the rock drawing of the Magdalenian draughtsmen.[27]

Eliot's artistic persona defers to the artistic tradition. If Eliot's poet is to remain relevant beyond their youth a relationship must exist between the individual and their "intellectual tradition."[28] We may interpret this relationship to take the form of an implicit contract, not unlike the social contract proposed by Jean Jacques Rousseau that mediates between the individual and society by providing a context for actions while articulating expectations for conduct. Rousseau proposes that moral freedom, that virtue acquired with civil society, allows man to become master of himself.[29] Without the social contract Rousseau says that the individual has the freedom to do absolutely anything he or she desires. The contract mediates between individual desires and those of others by acknowledging the abstract entity of civil society. Without some form of social contract, freedom to act is governed by the strength to impose one's will. With the social contract in place, the freedom of the individual to do absolutely anything he or she pleases is restrained, thus establishing civil rules of engagement between individuals.

In architectural terms the analog to Rousseau's social contract can be seen to be embodied in the notion of convention. Convention establishes ties to tradition and forms the ground upon which invention and departure from tradition can be understood. As Pelikan points out, first principles and insight are rediscovered through repetition, recitation, and reiteration of convention. Drawing the Orders, for example, can be seen as the architectural equivalent to recitation. The activity does not advance the polemic of architecture; rather it sets the stage for discourse and forms the foundation for insight into tradition. Like mastering the scales on the piano, the repetition of drawing provides mechanical skills as well as both verbal and non-verbal insights into the traditions which may presumably manifest themselves with the maturing of the artist. Without an education in convention, the student is condemned to illiteracy and the tyranny of the limits of their personal knowledge. However, through an education in convention, one is liberated from personal limitations. For Jacques Barzun, freedom to explore, to gain knowledge, to think abstractly or even pragmatically derives from the very notion of convention. Barzun points out that without convention even the simplest mechanical activities become impossible. Barzun's alphabetic convention parallels Rousseau's social contract; once the convention is mastered and understood, its application becomes limitless.

Within the tradition of Western architecture, a form of contract can be said to have been embodied in a conventional understanding of three essential areas: architectural elements, typology, and the city. Common educational experience formed an implicit contract between architects. Architects came to understand the issues of proportion, construction, and ornament through study of architectural elements. Principles of composition mediated the relationship between architectural elements and established the grounds for a formal typology that was never entirely independent of use. A common understanding of origins provided by typology fostered a shared vision of the ultimate architectural enterprise: the city. This vision was possible because of the existence of conventions for the deployment of elements and types. Convention produced a contract between individual architects, members of their intellectual society, the tradition of their craft, and the civic society that they served.

If tradition can be rediscovered as Pelikan suggests, then one might expect to find evidence of its rediscovery in the work of architects from one generation to the next. As an illustration of the rediscovery of tradition, we might look to the work of Le Corbusier. A superficial examination of this heroic modern figure might suggest little in the way of ties to tradition, but upon closer scrutiny it is quite apparent that Le Corbusier never completely severed his ties with the past. Even in his own words, the Alsatian architect admitted that the past was not to be discarded: "Though I have to admit that my own hands are soiled by the scourings of the past centuries, I prefer washing them to having them cut off. Besides, the centuries have not soiled our hands. Far from it they have filled them."[30]

While creating distance between the architect and tradition may have been on the agenda of many modern architects, it is clear that the most prolific spokesman of the new movement did not hold a point of view that was simple and reductive. Le Corbusier's sketchbooks, process drawings, writings, paintings, and built works represent the labors of an architect attempting to come to terms with the complexities presented by tradition seen in the context of modernity. The Pavilion de l'Esprit Nouveau of 1925, can be seen as evidence of the architect assimilating the principles of spatial organization that he observed and recorded in his own sketch book during a visit to the Carthusian Monastery of Ema. His seminal text, *Vers une Architecture*, pairs off the Parthenon, the church of Sta. Maria in Cosmedin, and most of Pompeii, on one side, and the Farman "Goliath," Delage automobiles, and great ocean liners on the other. For Le Corbusier the images of new technological inventions, the icons of modernity, were equivalent to the icons of tradition.

Le Corbusier realized that the material of art is never quite the same when he said, "There is a new spirit: it is a spirit of construction and synthesis guided by a clear conception."[31] He rejects the notion that art is progressive by asserting that "there is no such thing as primitive man; there are primitive resources."[32] Le Corbusier was certainly skeptical about "blind or timid adherence" to the successes of tradition:

> The lesson of Rome is for wise men, for those who know and can appreciate, who can resist and verify. Rome is the damnation of the half-educated. To send architectural students to Rome is to cripple them for life. The Grand Prix

The Five Orders of Architecture, after Vignola.

Though he viewed himself in the company of great architects of the past, he provided a hint that architecture is not simply the production of the labors of great individuals. He suggested that the type of architecture which he proposed was subject to abstract standards:

> The Parthenon is a product of selection applied to an established standard ...[36]

> ... Architecture is governed by standards. Standards are a matter of logic, analysis, and precise study. Standards are based on a problem which has been well stated. Architecture means plastic invention, intellectual speculation, higher mathematics.[37]

Unlike some of his contemporaries who sought to dispose of pre-existing traditions in order to enable an expression of their personal interpretation of the spirit of the age, Le Corbusier indicates his willingness to re-negotiate the contract through a re-definition of its terms. In order to address this, the concluding point of his argument returns to the suggestion that the terms provided by the original contract with tradition can be represented by a conventional understanding of three areas: architectural elements, typology, and the city.

One of the paradoxes surrounding much of the modern movement in architecture was the inability of its theorists to identify the responsibilities that would accompany the new freedoms that were to be accorded modern architects. Le Corbusier made several attempts throughout his career to codify the essential characteristics of the new architecture; advice that was no doubt intended for the responsible architect to heed. The Five Points, the Maison Dom-ino, and the Ville Contemporaine can be seen as attempts to supersede or replace the authority of the Five Orders and the assumptions of their traditional usage.

The Five Orders had enjoyed a reign over much of architectural discourse for nearly two millennia by evolving throughout

de Rome and the Villa Medici are the cancer of French architecture.[33]

Le Corbusier also realized that he would be measured and judged against the great figures of the past. He rather cleverly asserts that he is the missing figure in a very honorable trio when he says,[34] "Michael Angelo is the man of the last thousand years as Phidias was the man of the thousand years before."[35]

the course of history and adapting to the particulars of location, culture, and cosmological conception. The study of the Orders introduced students to the principles of style, proportion, and construction. Any attempt to supplant the usage of the classical orders presented no small task. Regardless, the abandonment of the classical system in favor of the less refined and untested polemic of modernity had serious consequences upon the fabric of architectural discourse.

Le Corbusier's Five Points—consisting of piloti, roof terraces, free plan, strip window, and free facade—can be seen as antidotes to the Five Orders. Though not as codified in terms of the relationship of the parts as were the Doric, Ionic, or Corinthian, Le Corbusier presented a hierarchical sequence of elements which connected generalized principles with specific formal associations. Unlike many of his contemporaries who asserted a series of principles of the new architecture, Le Corbusier was careful not to overgeneralize.[38] He continually refined and demonstrated the usage of these five principles through his built work and projects. We may intuit that his treatise on architecture is not confined to the single volume of *Vers une Architecture* but that it extends to the eight volumes of his *Oeuvre Complete*, numerous other writings, and his built work.

The second major term of the contract with tradition can be found in the manner in which the elements of architecture were combined to produce buildings. Laugier's primitive hut can be seen as an illustration of the traditional paradigm for the orchestration of architectural elements. The hut illustrates a convention that columns rest upon the ground; that columns support beams; that one needs four columns to support a roof and define a space. Laugier's hut composed of columns and Violet le Duc's hut composed of woven surfaces, a predecessor of the wall, present a myth of origins: "the problem well stated." The 1914 drawing of the Maison Dom-ino can be interpreted as Le Corbusier's substitution for Laugier or Violet le Duc's models. The Maison Dom-ino is not so much a design for a house as it is a diagram of its own compositional and constructional intentions. The famous

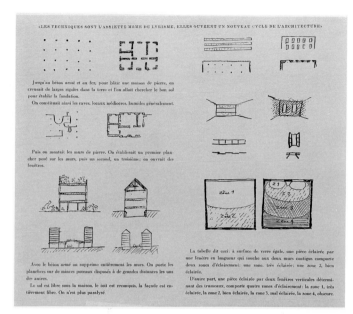

Le Corbusier, The Five Points of the New Architecture.

three-quarter view diagram strips away all reference to character and isolates a fundamental problem that had plagued academic architecture since the widespread introduction of the structural frame construction. Here with "the problem well stated" we learn, as the young architect does in the Laugier drawing, a set of fundamental principles that govern the relationships between architectural elements. In the Maison Dom-ino, Le Corbusier explores an image of a type which like Laugier's hut establishes its authority on the basis of natural reason. Le Corbusier did not, however, end his search for the development of a typological basis for architecture with a notion of origins alone.

J.N.L. Durand's, *Recueil et Parallel e des Edifices de Tout Genre, Anciens et Moderns*, provides an illustration of what Kenneth Frampton suggests was, "an architectural counterpart to the Napoleonic Code."[39] Unlike the Primitive Hut/Dom-ino notion of type as an elucidation of first principles, Durand's notion of type connects physical form to a rationalist understanding of social, cultural and economic conditions. In that sense,

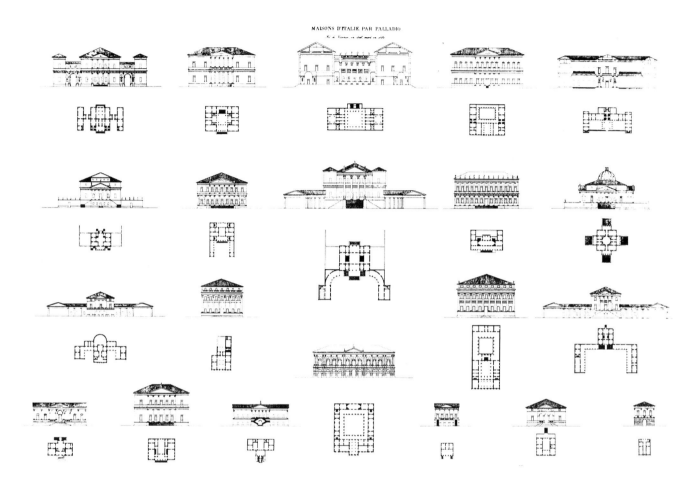

J.N.L. Durand, Maisons D'Italie par Palladio.

Durand's notion of type is closer to that of Quatremere de Quincey, the originator of the notion of typology, who saw the type as a physical manifestation of cultural phenomena and institutionalized memory.

In his *Oeuvre Complete*, Le Corbusier presents a series of formal generalizations concerning his own built work, on the page directly following the 1929 version of the Villa Savoye. These are illustrated through a series of diagrams derived from the Maison La Roche-Jeanneret, the Villa at Garches, the Weissenhof House modeled on the Citrohan House, and the Villa at Poissy. They represent typological strategies for formal design. Not surprisingly the most restrained type, that proposed by Garches, is deemed "most difficult," while the most Miesian of the four, the type derived from house at Stuttgart, is judged to be the "easiest." The first diagram in the sequence presents a very malleable perimeter and is no doubt intended as a response to the difficult conditions of site. The type modeled after the Villa at Garches is indicative of the quintessential background building, still very difficult to make. It was probably intended to serve as a model for the Redent Housing which Le Corbusier proposed in his urban schemes. The latter two represent versions, at least in their diagrams, of the penetrable perimeter (Weissenhof) and the fixed perimeter (Villa Savoye) both as models for the object building. In a similar light, we may view the Citrohan House itself as not being the product of pure invention, an expression of the Zeitgeist; rather we can view it as belonging to an interpretation of the row house, an established type. Likewise, the Villa at Garches, the Villa Savoye, or the Palace of the Assembly at Chandigarh can be seen as engaging a pre-established architectural tradition of typology. In actual practice, these typologies remain surprisingly conventional when viewed in the context of the traditional city. The Maison Planex of 1927 or the Maison Cook of 1926, both built in Parisian suburbs, defer to the hierarchy of their urban situation and exhibit sophisticated contextual responses to their respective neighborhoods. They illustrate the capacity of modern architecture to establish a harmonious coexistence with their more traditional neighbors. These two buildings ably illustrate what Michael Dennis stated in his book, *Court and Garden*: that modern architecture, though revolutionary in appearance, was evolutionary in principle.[40]   It is apparent that both the Maison Planex and the Maison Cook were, in their day, polemically energized in terms of their iconography and style, while they represent rather benign and conventional insights in terms of their typologies.

Le Corbusier did not merely reiterate or recover the typologies of the past, rather he exercised his insight gained from an intensive examination of architectural traditions. Both Colin Rowe's article, "Mathematics of the Ideal Villa," and Kurt Forster's article, "Antiquity and Modernity in the LaRoche and Jeanneret Houses of 1929," provide strong indications that Le Corbusier reinterpreted established typologies through his design process, thereby reconstituting a portion of the contract with tradition. The notion of typology related to the Maison Dom-ino is distinct from the notion of typology displayed by the later parallel of

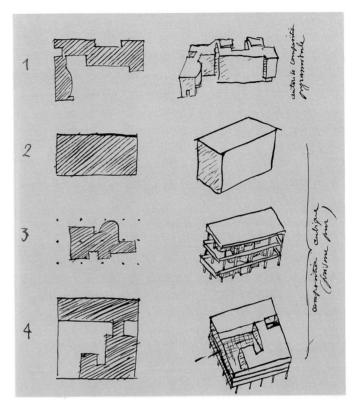

Le Corbusier, Les 4 Compositions.

architectural projects. The Dom-ino is an illustration of an internally referential notion of type. It is a codification of parts and their inter-relationships based upon principles internal to the discipline of architecture. On the other hand, the notion of type displayed by both Durand and the Le Corbusier drawings constitutes an understanding that is informed and engaged in diverse external criteria: cultural, societal, and economic conditions. Failure to pay attention to the former type may result in a poorly constructed, syntactically garbled or weakly composed building, while ignorance of the later type may result in a building that is unintelligible, unconventional and unusable. One of the lines of inquiry in Rowe's article deals with the distinction between natural and customary beauty. An appreciation of natural beauty is inherently understood geometrically while a taste for custom-

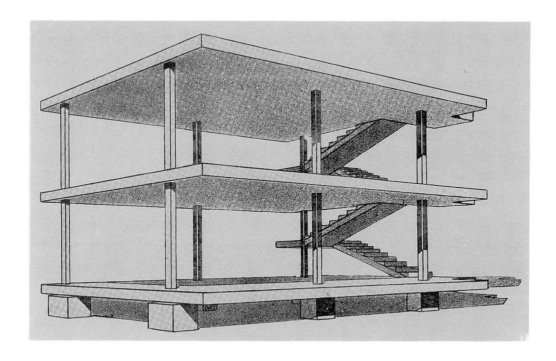

Le Corbusier, Maison Dom-ino.

ary beauty is acquired.[41] The Dom-ino may illustrate the connection with the notion of natural beauty; the relationships are geometric and internally referential.[42]   On the other hand, because these diagrams are informed by conditions external to architecture, the parallel of building projects can be seen as illustrations of customary beauty.   In short, Le Corbusier's adoption of a notion of typology that takes into account conditions that are both internal and external to the discipline forms a bridge between the particularities of the element and the general conditions of the city.

The final clause of the covenant with tradition concerns the manner in which buildings are orchestrated in the context of the city. Sabastiano Serlio's Tragic, Comic, and Satyric stage sets can be invoked to represent the tradition of making cities handed down through generations of architects. The Tragic scene might represent the address of the aristocracy; the Comic scene could depict the merchant class; while the Satyric scene gives view to the trials and tribulations of the happy peasantry. Curiously, Le

Corbusier includes three similarly formatted perspectives in his *Oeuvre Complete* presentation of the 1922 Ville Contemporaine. With a new social order in place the Tragic scene of Serlio can be reconstituted as a view of the city from the *autostrada*. The Comic scene finds its counterpart in a depiction of a street of *redents*. The Satyric scene is accordingly addressed in the view from the cafés into the grand civic gardens.

While the typical client of Le Corbusier was in fact bourgeois and necessitated some conventional grounding in type, the urban client was presumably classless, a condition that certainly never existed in Le Corbusier's day. Though tragically flawed, the Ville Contemporaine, the Plan Voisin, and even Chandigarh represent the architect's concern over establishing standards for urbanism which in this case can clearly be understood as departures from, or even inversions, of tradition.

Le Corbusier concluded his text, *Vers une Architecture,* with the much quoted challenge, "Architecture or Revolution," to which he adds, "Revolution can be avoided," as a refrain.[43]

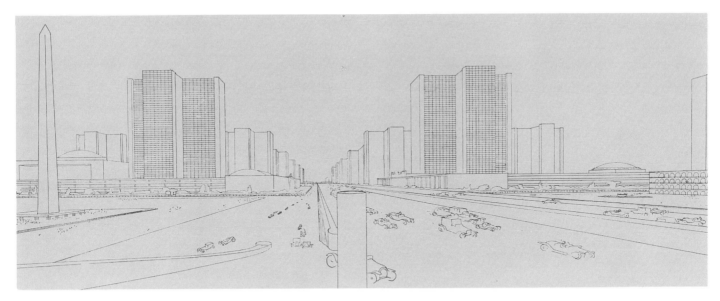

Le Corbusier, Une Ville Contemporaine.

Standardization was to provide the terms of the new contract which would enable the individual architect to operate in the context of his or her peers, tradition, and culture. The existence of a re-negotiated contract would provide the means to avoid the revolution. Because Le Corbusier's contract with tradition exhibits serious flaws at the scale of the city does not mean that all modern urbanism was similarly problematic. However, Le Corbusier's problems with urbanism might imply that his insights into traditions of the city were flawed. Berlage's plan for Amsterdam South of 1915, or the Cancellotti, et. al., plan for Sabaudia of 1934 are but two examples of modern urbanism wherein the contract with tradition underwent successful reconstitution.

While it might be possible, even in certain circumstances desirable, to design and build an architectural element or an individual building by disregarding or subverting convention, the enterprise of making the city is another matter altogether. Like the society it supports, the city grants individuals rights in return for

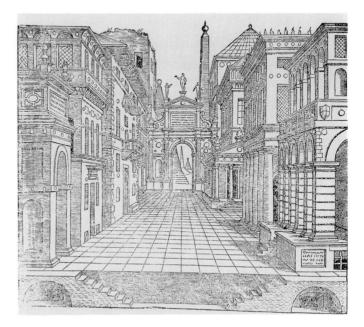

Sabastiano Serlio, The Tragic Scene.

their responsible action. Freedom is understood within the symmetrical context of right versus responsibility. Outside of that context there exists only the freedom to impose one's will predicated upon strength, be it physical, economic, or political. However inadequate, vehicles have been developed to describe the rights of the individual landowner as well as his or her responsibilities toward the legal entity of the city. Coding, zoning, and covenants are all tools for defining a context for freedom. Artistic freedom, on the other hand, is not as rigorously defined. Occasionally ordinances or other legal apparatus have been enacted to insure a certain character or preserve a particular historic tradition, but broad legal authority over artistic matters, at least in America, has never been quite palatable. The responsibility for such matters has typically rested in the academy.

The genesis of the academy in the European context can be seen as an extension of the authority of the crown over artistic matters. The centrally managed *Beaux Arts* system in France insured that students enrolled in a provincial *école* were given an education that was compatible with that of a counterpart in Paris. In colonial and imperial terms, the academy was an essential tool for extending the presence of the crown to distant parts of the world. Throughout Southeast Asia, Africa, and parts of the New World, cities and particularly their major public buildings attest to the effectiveness of the French Academy.

In North America, centralized federal authority over education never existed as it had in Europe, yet the model of the French academy proved to be an important element in the training of young architects. While the social contract in America had been reconstructed through the United States Constitution, the recognition of a conventional American architecture was to lag behind. Jefferson's plans for the grounds of the University of Virginia can be seen as an introduction of modern architectural principles and civic values to the United States. While significant, the University of Virginia plan was to be limited in its direct impact on the architecture and urbanism in the new country. The purchase of the French territories and its subsequent partitioning by the Continental Congress in 1785 formed a more important and explicit convention for urbanism than any single architectural development. Operating under the urgent need to occupy territory, to subdue and claim the landscape as part of the new nation, the building types and construction methods employed on the frontier were typically not the products of the academy. Craft traditions that had been passed down from father to son were largely employed to form the first generation of urban fabric in the Louisiana Purchase. Finding architectural discourse in America to be limited, Richard Morris Hunt, then H. H. Richardson and others, sought an education in Paris and brought European sophistication back to their native country. With the establishment of architecture schools in America, it was not surprising to see that many eventually patterned themselves after the model of the *École des Beaux Arts*.

The mission of the modern university is perhaps two-fold: to preserve knowledge and resist change while simultaneously seeking knowledge and instigating change. This dual mission institutionalizes a critical attitude towards tradition and its reconstitution from one generation to the next. When one or the other of these components is abandoned, the contract with tradition risks becoming severed. Perhaps Andres Duany and Elizabeth Plater-Zyberk's (DPZ) Architectural Code for new towns such as Seaside, Florida can be seen as evidence of the result in an imbalance in the mission of the academy. The Seaside Code would have been unnecessary to architects at the turn of the century. The intentions of the urban plan were easily understood by means of its conventions, and architects easily proposed variations on the theme without additional restraint. DPZ's new town codes seek to achieve an understanding of convention that typically would have been instilled in the environment of the academy.

The DPZ attitude towards convention can be seen in direct contrast to Robert Venturi's attitude expressed in *Learning from Las Vegas*.[44] Though indeed the rediscovery, or recovery of small town planning principles exhibited in the work of DPZ derive from similar methods to the "case studies" that resulted in Venturi's urban manifesto, the attitude toward architecture and urbanism is decidedly different. Venturi embraces the notion of architecture and urbanism as a mirror of the present predicament; giving license to the vulgarities of the strip.[45] He attempts to elevate the mundane to the level of the heroic through glorification of "the ugly and the ordinary." Duany and Plater-Zyberk, on the other hand, look toward the "beautiful and the extraordinary."[46] The distilled architectural and urban traditions of the new-town code in the DPZ model are a lamp to guide the architect through the difficult process of design, a restraining device against vulgarity.

Both positions, however, seem inadequate in establishing a context for freedom. Venturi's position lends itself to the law of appetite: the biggest most vulgar "duck" or "decorated shed" gets all of the attention. And while the DPZ model may be understood as a prescription for freedom through obedience to law, one cannot help but wonder why this form of post-graduate tutorial should be necessary at all. Were the dual missions of the academy in balance, architects would be making architecture and cities as a result of a shared notion of convention. Modern society and culture have been preoccupied with the "relationship between the exception and the rule or, in other terms, the relation between transgression and normative commitment."[47] Only when one participates in the process of enacting the rules does one perceive the merits of the rule or its transgression. In American Society participation in the formation of the rules is one of the few instances where the notion of right and responsibility converge.

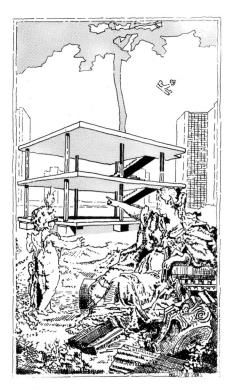

The New Contract.

NOTES

1 Jean Jaques Rousseau, *The Social Contract* (New York: Penguin Books, 1968), 65.

2 Jacques Barzun, *The House of Intellect* (New York: Harper and Brothers, 1959), 6.

3 David Watkin, *Morality and Architecture: The Development of a Theme in Architectural History and Theory from the Gothic Revival to the Modern Movement* (Chicago: The University of Chicago Press, 1977), 113.

4 Ernst Gombrich, *In Search of Cultural History* (Oxford: Clarendon Press, 1969), 6.

5 Gombrich, *Cultural History*, 8.

6 Gombrich, *Cultural History*, 10.

7 Gombrich, *Cultural History*, 10.

8 Gombrich, *Cultural History*, 15.

9 Had Burkhardt lived to chronicle the culture of twentieth century America, he no doubt would have maintained an affinity with the character of the "Monday morning quarterback."

10 Peter Burke, *The Italian Renaissance: Culture and Society in Italy* (Princeton: Princeton University Press, 1986), 3-4.

11 Burke suggests "...an open social history which explores connections between culture and society without assuming that the imaginary is determined by economic or social forces." *The Italian Renaissance*, 4.

12 Karl Popper, *The Poverty of Historicism* (New York: Harper and Row, 1964), 150.

13 John Meunier, "Architecture and the Zeitgeist," *Central* (Cincinatti: University of Cincinatti, et. al., Spring 1980), 45-46. In his review of Watkin's book, John Meunier notes that Watkin, ironically, may be guilty of embracing a particular movement by becoming both supporter and spokesman. With the advantage of time on our side, finding Watkin in the circle of H.R.H. Charles today might substantiate Meunier's claim and reinforce Gombrich: "... Burkhardt here illustrates the important methodological truth that it is precisely those people who want to discard all 'preconceived' theories who are most likely uncon-

sciously to succumb to their power." (Gombrich, *Cultural History*,14.)

14 'What is important for our purposes is the clear assumption that there is a 'spirit' or 'essence' which pervades and dominates all intellectual, artistic, and social activity. Artists are not individuals with unique imaginations and talents, but are only manifestations of this all-pervasive spirit or essence." (Watkin, *Morality and Architecture*, 75).

15 Colin Rowe refers to this technophilia as "physics envy" in his article, "The Present Urban Predicament," *Cornell Journal of Architecture 1* (New York: Rizzoli), 17. We might imagine the logical conclusion of a Hegelian manipulation of history producing circumstances comparable to that of an engineer in his relationship to the calculation of the forces of structure. Hegel no doubt hoped that historical processes could assist in prediction of the future. Both engineers and historians measure forces that are not readily apparent to the eye. Through their methodology, they predict the parameters and the behavior of physical structures. Were the Hegelian model correct we would no doubt benefit from a new class of historian/engineers.

16 Watkin, *Morality and Architecture* , 43.

17 Watkin, *Morality and Architecture*, 43.

18 T.S. Eliot, "Tradition and the Individual Talent," *Selected Essays* (New York: Harcourt Brace Jovanovich, 1964), 6.

19 Eliot, "Tradition and the Individual Talent," 4.

20 Eliot, "Tradition and the Individual Talent," 4.

21 Jaroslav Pelikan, *The Vindication of Tradition*, (New Haven: The Yale University Press,1984), 65.

22 Pelikan, *Vindication of Tradition*, 65.

23 Pelikan, *Vindication of Tradition*, 73.

24 Pelikan, *Vindication of Tradition*, 76.

25 Pelikan, *Vindication of Tradition*, 72.

26 Eliot, "Tradition and the Individual Talent," 5.

27 Eliot, "Tradition and the Individual

Talent," 6.

28 Many cultures enact rites of passage that articulate the expectations that are associated with acts of adulthood and differentiate these actions from the tolerated capricious behavior of youth. Connected with the "freedoms" of adulthood are an equally understood set of "responsibilities" and expectations concerning both the actions of the individual and his or her relationship to society. "Coming of age" carries with it the notion that one is held responsible for understanding and upholding the "social contract", that abstract "other" which permits civil society to exist.

29 Rousseau, *The Social Contract*, 65.

30 W. Boesiger and O. Stonorov, *Le Corbusier et Pierre Jeanneret Oeuvre Complete 1910-29* (Zurich: Les Editions d'Architecture,1964), 11.

31 Le Corbusier, *Towards a New Architecture*, Frederick Etchells, trans. (New York: Holt, Rinehart and Winston, 1960), 101.

32 Le Corbusier, *Towards a New Architecture*, 66.

33 Le Corbusier, *Towards a New Architecture*, 161.

34 Colin Rowe has suggested that Le Corbusier saw himself in the role of the figure of the millennium.

35 Le Corbusier, *Towards a New Architecture,* 116.

36 Le Corbusier, *Towards a New Architecture*, 23.

37 Le Corbusier, *Towards a New Architecture*, 137-138.

38 The De Stijl Manifesto contained nine clauses; Theo van Doesburg articulated 16 points in his Towards a Plastic Architecture; the Sant'Elia and Marinetti opposed and despised four separate categories of architectural theory and proclaimed allegiance to eight others. See Ulrich Conrad's *Programs and Manifestos on 20th Century Architecture* (Cambridge, Massachusetts: MIT Press,1964).

39 Kenneth Frampton, *Modern Architecture* (New York: Oxford, 1980), 15.

40 Michael Dennis, *Court and Garden:*

From the French Hôtel to the City of Modern Architecture (Cambridge: MIT Press, 1986). In particular see Chapter 7, "Architecture and the Cumulative City."

41 Colin Rowe, "Mathematics of the Ideal Villa," *Mathematics of the Ideal Villa and Other Essays* (Cambridge: MIT Press,1976), 2.

42 For a discussion of the Maison Domino as a self referential apparatus see Peter Eisenman, "Aspects of Modernism: Maison Dom-ino and the Self Referential Sign," *Oppositions 15/16* (Cambridge: MIT Press,1980), 129.

43 Eisenman, "Aspects of Modernism," 269.

44 Historian Vincent Scully wrongly identified Venturi as the father of the "New Urbanism" in his talk "An Urbanism for Our Time," delivered at the First Congress for the New Urbanism, held in Alexandria, Virginia, October 9, 1993. While one might credit Venturi for his contribution to the rediscovery of architectural traditions in *Complexity and Contradiction*, his position on urbanism, like that of Le Corbusier, is antithetical to traditional urbanism. In fact, Venturi's attitude concerning resistance to the forces of the anti-urban model of Las Vegas is, "if you can't beat them then join them!"

45 This is not to say that Venturi's Las Vegas is without its rules; they operate, however, as a result of the topsy-turvey world of carnival. Las Vegas is the product of Pop Culture, whereas Duany and Plater-Zyberk's interests lie in the arena of traditional culture.

46 Duany and Plater-Zyberk's initial ideas concerning small-town planning principles derive in part from an intensive examination of towns in the Southern portion of the United States. Like Venturi's case study method in Learning from Las Vegas, DPZ observed, documented, and analyzed the predicament of the small-town in an attempt to distill its salient principles.

47 Dominick LaCapra, *Soundings in Critical Theory* (Ithaca, New York: Cornell University Press, 1989), 17-18.

FIGURE CREDITS

Frontis Marc-Antione Laugier, *An Essay on Architecture* (Los Angeles: Hennessey and Ingalls, 1977).

1 Arthur Lyman Tuckerman, *The Five Orders of Architecture According to Giacomo Barrozi di Vignola* (New York: Wm. T. Comstock, 1896). Permission granted by Research Publications International.

2 Le Corbusier, *Le Corbusier et Pierre Jeanneret Ouvre Complete: 1910-29.* © 1994 Artists Rights Society (ARS), New York/SPADEM, Paris.

3 J.N.L. Durand, *Recueil et Parallel e des Edifices de Tout Genre, Anciens et Moderns* (Bruxelles, 1842).

4-6 Le Corbusier, *Ouvre Complete: 1910-29.* ©1994 ARS, New York/ SPADEM, Paris.

7 Sebastiano Serlio, *The Five Books of Architecture.*

8 Courtesy of the author.

YOUR AESTHETIC INTERESTS ARE SECURE:
DESIGN CONTROL AND THE GATE-GUARDED COMMUNITY

FRANK EDGERTON MARTIN
PHOTOGRAPHS BY CHRISTOPHER FAUST

Frank Edgerton Martin and Christopher Faust are founding members of the Suburban Documentation Project, a non-profit research and educational organization based in Minneapolis.

Freedom's here. And security too. Not locks on top of locks, but highly professional security. All access to the residential areas is limited to security gates 24 hours a day, every day of the year.

The aesthetic integrity of your community is also secure. A committee of architects, land planners and engineers has established criteria defining setbacks, fences, height limitations, and construction materials, as well as landscape themes and materials.

Each home at Castle Pines Village must be approved by the Design Review Committee. There is variety and creativity to be sure. Above all there is quality.

Castle Pines Village, promotional portfolio, 1993[1]

Gatehouse under construction at Glen Oaks, May 1993.

In the 1990s, the tension between individual rights and the good of the whole pose a continuing challenge in the planning of American communities, schools, and information networks. Even when the rate of violent crime is actually declining in many regions, the local television news, marketed to suburban demographics, feeds fears of urban anarchy with nightly images of shootings, fires and drug deals taking place in minority communities. White collar crime, much less likely to make good video, remains far more invisible in the selective observation of modern dangers to civility.

Traditional democratic space has been shaped by the necessary struggle between individual liberties and collective security. Yet in the elite suburbs of our time the obsession with security, with gate-houses, guards and motion detectors now includes strict control of residential and landscape design. This kind of design control requires an entirely new layer of voluntary governance that exists outside of traditional public agencies. In 1993, the New York Times reported that more than "32 million Americans—nearly one in eight—now live in some form of homeowners association...."[2]

Gate-guarded communities such as Castle Pines outside of Denver and Des Moines' Glen Oaks represent a new refinement of social control in the guise of design review. The architect, when hired to plan such developments and their design restrictions serves as a new kind of cop—an environmental security force for the nouveau gentry at the urban fringe. The literature produced to promote these new communities is telling: the perception of safety in the rich suburbs of our time comes as much from the tastefully contextual roof line as from the rapid police response.

FEAR AS A DESIGN PROBLEM

In a recent *Metropolis* article, Karrie Jacobs writes of the booming "fear industry that targets consumers who are still relatively insulated from violence, who believe that a few minor adjustments, a fine-tuning of their life-style, will give them the safety that society no longer affords. This is fear as a design problem."[3] The profusion of new gated communities throughout the West and Midwest provide not only a physical, but an aesthetic solution for relieving the upset caused by the "passionate intemperance of city life." The presence of guards, home security systems, personal security alarms are a not so subtly-coded answer to fear.

Yet this hardware is no more important than the architectural coding of historicism, summer resorts, English names and the suggestion of happier times. Electronic surveillance works in tandem with an architectural veneer of dentils, coins, hipped roofs, turrets and carriage lamps. For those who can afford it, this high-tech/nostalgic mix seems to testify that design can solve social problems, or at least, keep them at bay.

This replacement of products for trust, of urban simulacrum for civility, threatens to place many architects and planners in the security business. "It is a shift," Jacobs argues, "away from the idea that we live surrounded by governmental agencies and social structures that will protect us from harm—environmental and health hazards as well as crime—and towards the idea that we live on a lawless frontier where only our own cunning and self-interest will keep us safe."[4]

Ironically, suburbs were once secondary places located outside of the gates of the city, the territory of the disenfranchised, naked to the dangers of the wilderness. The suburbs of the 1990s respond to a different wilderness: the perceived vice and violence that so increasingly characterizes the inner city.[5] Before their re-emergence in the late 1980s and 90s, gated streets could be found in the new neighborhoods of late nineteenth century St. Louis, Boston and Chicago.

Conceived in the 1850s on the basis of a rural villa, Llewellyn Park in New Jersey was among the nation's first limited-access master-planned communities. Alluding to picturesque ideals with ravines, rock outcroppings and other trappings of a "beautiful brokenness of scenery," the 750 acre site rivalled Central Park in size while offering expansive views to New York City and the ocean. The development centered on a fifty-acre ramble, whose entrance was monitored by an inhabited gate-house. The home sites ranged from one to twenty acres and were linked by sinuous carriage roads. Visitors were required to write down their names in a registry held at the gate-house. On Sundays, however, the gates were locked so that residents could appreciate the romantic, barren wilds creeping up their backyards.

HOUSES AS PRODUCTS

"Suburbia in the Nineties has a logo," wrote David Guterson in his description of the master-planned Green Valley community outside Las Vegas; a "town" with several neighborhoods of varying economic strata.[6] Numerous regulations controlling both access and aesthetics create a unique insularity that renders such communities as commodities. Careful observers will note, "the southwest's pastel palette coloring a community devoid of improvisation, of caprice, spontaneity, effusiveness, or the charm of error—of a place where the process of commodification has at last leached life of the accidental and ecstatic, the divine, reckless and enraged."[7] The implication here may be that a life (and a landscape) without accidents, digressions of taste, silly acts and surprises is also a life and a place without spirit.

In response to the confusing people and symbols of modern life, many Americans move to the new suburbs to recapture for themselves the predictability and homogeneity that has been lost in mass culture. It *is* possible to buy a home on a street, in a neighborhood and legal framework where everyone agrees with you about the colors and tableaus that are appropriate for a home and a community. Yet, as new developments age, an increasing number of its residents might find themselves dissatisfied with the status quo, such as the Seattle family who, after years of compliance with the conventional earth tones of their neighborhood, decided to paint their house purple. As reported by the *New York Times*, the family was chastised and eventually sued by the homeowners association for their aesthetic violation of the palette:

> What happened to the Jones family is one of the more unusual conflicts from the world of private governments that control numerous details of daily living in suburbs, town houses and condominiums. When people move to the suburbs they often say that they are looking for safety and a certain homogeneity. What Lee and Barbara Jones say they found with their dream home was a repressiveness bordering on tyranny.[8]

As an ongoing survey of contemporary metropolitan landscapes, we at the Suburban Documentation Project photograph the emergence of gated communities as exemplars of perceived fear and social stratification in contemporary America. We study these new suburban landscapes not only as evidence of human hopes, but as concrete expressions of how Americans define such ideals as freedom, community, nature, and security through the transformation of the landscape.

The Suburban Documentation Project began in 1990 as a collaboration between a photographer and a landscape architect who use the visual force of photography and analytical methods of design research to stimulate public discussion over contemporary suburban growth. Based in Minneapolis, the Project is currently expanding its scope to include photo-documentation of the Des Moines, Chicago, Kansas City, Omaha and Denver regions through the assistance of local planners, design professionals and historians.

Over the last four years the Suburban Documentation Project has witnessed and recorded the explosion of historicism in recent suburban house designs and the wasteful use of open land that characterizes American development shaped by the car. Although rarely documented in the visual arts or discussed in architectural theory, new suburbs provide some of the purest geographic expressions of the environmental values of our era.

Our visits to the following three gate-guarded communities capture the physical environment at various stages of development and explore the nature of covenants, homeowners associations and other forms of design control. Our premise is that gated communities, marketed with allusions to ideal pasts and ideal settings, are sold with an underlying code of fear.

A PREPONDERANCE OF DECORATIVE BRICK: GLEN OAKS IN DES MOINES

> *The Glen Oaks gate-guarded master plan community concept provides privacy and an added element of security within the open, rolling hills of the grounds.... Home sites are available in one quarter and one third acre lots, and homes priced from $300,000 to $500,000+ will have a unified appearance through traditional architectural themes, with a preponderance of decorative brick, wood roofings and custom windows.*[9]

With slender and elegant streets that weave through wood lots and rolling hills, Glen Oaks is a 511-acre limited-access golf and country club being developed fifteen miles west of Des Moines, Iowa. Beginning in the spring of 1993, we photographed the development at two times: in the pristine moment after the streets were newly paved and the earth freshly graded—and again in the fall when trees had been planted and model houses begun.

The promotional portfolio from Glen Oaks includes a project description, membership information, color site plans, lot prices, newsletter, a club application and personal reference form. Also included in the package is a typed "Lot Buyer's Questions and Answers" that explain the Homeowners Association and the all important Declaration of Covenants, Conditions and Restrictions, or "CC&Rs." These restraints are the heart of the environmental control of the architecture and commonly-held space in Glen Oaks. The sheet also outlines minimum requirements for home sizes—a complicated formula that, in the final sum, allows no house to have less than 2,200 square feet of finished area, construction time limits, a total restriction of satellite dishes, boats and campers in public view, and the stipulation that, "Any external pet structure will be subject to approval by the Architectural Review Committee and will need to be fully screened from the street, adjacent lots and golf course."[10]

In describing the entry drive to the development, the Glen Oaks newsletter boasts that,

> With the introduction of specimen oak trees, wooden hurdle fences, stone columns, and the creation of a recirculation pond and natural stone waterfall feature, this entrance becomes a strong statement of the "natural" landscape theme that is so dominant throughout the residential and golf course communities within the Glen Oaks development. The use of native landscaping and natural rock outcroppings, directly relating to the character and construction of the Clubhouse and Tennis facilities, allow the south entrance at Glen Oaks to set the stage for members, residents, and guests for the overall golf community experience.[11]

At Glen Oaks, the Tom Fazio golf course is the marketing centerpiece for high-priced housing whose community planners and residential designers remain far less well-known. In the May 17, 1993 price list, lots designated as "Interior" averaged about $90,000 for 28,000 square feet with "Golf" lots ranging from $140,000 to $175,000. These relatively average-sized suburban lots cost as much as the typical house in the Des Moines real estate market. That this fairly remote land, so recently farmed, should command such prices testifies to the importance of the golf-course as an amenity.

In these environments, the home buyer's land purchase, construction costs and club membership can easily total $700,000. Even for the rapidly ascending executive, this kind of money is no small change. And though the contracts and the CC&Rs are very explicitly defined, buying into such a self-contained world means that one has also bought its fluid assumptions about tradition, equality, and nature.

When we revisited the site in October 1993, the natural stone waterfall feature was well underway and specimen trees had begun to appear in the center islands of the roads and around the gates.

CASTLE PINES VILLAGE: WHERE DENVER BECOMES COLORADO AGAIN

At day's end, as you sit on your patio, talking about shots made and shots missed, take a look up. You'll see a sky you haven't seen in years, with more stars than you can ever remember. Yes, even the sky is different here.[12]

Castle Pines is the site of the nationally-known Jack Nicklaus golf course where, in the late 1980s, RJR Nabisco executives hobnobbed, golfed and strategized a leveraged buy-out of their company. Now almost ten years old, this gated community is still advertised prominently in Colorado business magazines. Castle Pines boasts that it is three minutes south of downtown Denver and , more importantly, fifteen minutes away from the Denver Technology Park, one of the Edge Cities that rival downtown Denver as a center of high-paying jobs in the service economy.

Appropriately, one leaves I-25 and enters Castle Pines from Happy Canyon Road. Because of high security, our only chance of entering was to take a tour with a real estate agent. Instead, we opted to see the promotional video. We noted that both the video and the marketing literature contained the key phrase, "The aesthetic integrity of your community is also secure," the most honest linkage of the role of architecture and security we have seen to date.

In Castle Pines, not only is life more predictable but, if the marketing hype is to be believed, it is also more authentically Coloradan. As the place where "Denver Becomes Colorado Again," Castle Pines exists as the arcadian middle landscape. The development is appropriately touted as one of those rare places where the artifice of city life succumbs to the sublimity of nature.

As we have noted elsewhere, one of the great ironies of fringe development, whether for the rich or middle class, is that new growth generally destroys the scenic values that first drew people so far out into the country. Nonetheless, Castle Pines' mountain

Glen Oaks, Entry Drive. May 1993.

Glen Oaks, Entry Drive. October 1993.

views will remain safe from future visual blights if additional legal controls or outright ownership can be extended to protect the scenic resource. As major concentrations of wealth and tax base, the homeowners associations of gate-guarded communities will increasingly become powerful opponents to additional developments in their own backyards.

THE GOLDEN BEAR AND BEARPATH

At Bearpath, you can leave the troubles of the outside world behind as you enter the guarded stone gateway to your neighborhood.[13]

Minnesota's first "gate-guarded master-planned golf community" is now under construction in Eden Prairie, an affluent and rapidly growing suburb on the southwestern fringe of the Twin Cities with a commercial-industrial tax base that rivals that of many traditional urban centers. Located along Pioneer Trail, one of the oldest routes west along the Minnesota River bluffs, Bearpath promises to be, by 1998, an insular neighborhood of 295 homes. Surrounding the entire 420 acre site will be a fence to keep unwanted visitors out of neighboring properties and parks. Along Pioneer trail to the south, the perimeter fence will be wrought iron and placed on a planted berm. To the east, visitors will approach the gate along Dell Road, which will be rebuilt by the developer in brick and stone.

Like Castle Pines, the Bearpath golf course is designed by Jack Nicklaus. "With his meticulous attention to detail," the promotional newsletter "Bear Tracks" boasts, "Nicklaus and his Golden Bear International team of architects, agronomists, and designers will help transform 420 acres of rolling wilderness into his first golf course in Minnesota and one of the finest golf courses in the entire country."[14]

Glen Oaks. May 1993.

Glen Oaks. October 1993.

uth entrance, 1993.

Castle Pines. Promotional video, 1993.

Glen Oaks. S

Advertisement for Bearpath. Downtown Minneapolis, 1993.

Bearpath. Construction of streets, February 1994.

Bearpath. Construction of streets, February 1994.

Since the time of European settlement in the 1850s, Eden Prairie has contained neither wilderness nor bears. It seems that Bearpath's name, and its pastoral golf hole logo with a white bear peaking through cumulus clouds, have more to do with Nicklaus (known as "the Golden Bear" in the golf world) than any historic or ecological precedent. The sales center contains a Nicklaus pro-shop complete with the Nicklaus line of golf equipment. The sales staff look like golf pros and are uniformed in warm-up suits even on the coldest February days. After making an appointment, the visitor is taken out into the site in a black Jeep Cherokee with four-wheel drive traction that can handle a short, invigorating trek through muddy frontier conditions. The sales center itself is furnished with reproduction English furniture and carefully arranged old hardback books such as De Maupassant's *Short Stories of Life*.

Upon completion Bearpath will be not only a community, but a country club with a 30,000 square foot clubhouse and memberships offered on a priority basis to property owners. The "Questions and Answers about Bearpath Golf and Country Club Community" explains that all club memberships "are subject to the approval by Bearpath Golf and Country Club's Membership Committee. Bearpath Golf and Country Club will offer its members and guests a lifestyle that is complete and of superior quality."[15]

Bearpath, like its counterpart communities across the country, is protected not only by gates and home security technology, but by a network of watchful eyes in the form of one's neighbors, the Owners Association and its attorneys. Yet David Chapman, Bearpath's Executive Vice President, foresaw a community that would be truly diverse in its residents and their options to express themselves; "We expect that lots will go quickly. When we're finished, there will be a type of home for practically every taste.... We have lifestyles for everyone, and the real estate in this community will continue to appreciate in value."[16]

IMPLICATIONS FOR AMERICAN ENGLISH

As we continue to study how American ideals of home and community are expressed in new suburbs, we in the Suburban Documentation Project are concerned not only about the loss of farm land and pedestrian-oriented neighborhoods, but by the loss of a richness and clarity of language. Our continuing experience with the marketing of landscape and community ideals to the wealthy and their imitators reveals a counterbalancing poverty of language. The world of real estate and business finance encourages us to read the fine print. But the world of real estate marketing, of videos, brochures and historic tableaus, functions so well because most buyers rarely question the biggest print, the mythologies that envelop us so broadly as to become invisible. The Glen Oaks publications reassure us that residents will live in a "relaxed country club ambience rich in tradition."[17] However, what constitutes "tradition" and "ambience" is based on an unspoken consensus about sports, picturesque outcroppings and native plants. Like these verbal characterizations, the veneer of landscape and architectural ornament suggests a reconnection with nature and a desired past.

As much as our photos, our study of suburbs records the words and verbal images of real estate sales and promotion. We conclude here with questions of our own that have more to do with simple words than broad architectural trends.

Is human "diversity" really something that can be expressed through variations in house styles? When developers say they offer, "lifestyles for everyone," have they innocently forgotten the exclusionary costs of membership, or the contractual restrictions placed on such things as pet structures? Are "freedom" and "security" necessarily grounded in predictability and control? What does "freedom" mean in a community that no longer tolerates the free-flight of speech, public demonstration and the protection of minority voices?

The real implication here is that tasteful design and well-meaning environmentalism cannot atone for the growing segregation of metropolitan regions and a diminishing chance for the children of the future to meet other children who are different from themselves. The most elaborate stage set architecture and simulation technologies cannot alone create a sense of community, transcendence and wonder. "Security" as a word and as an ideal is no longer found in the extended family, one's spiritual life or trust in one's neighbors. It comes from a predictable landscape that is "safe", both through its walls, alarms and gates as well as its aesthetic assurances.

NOTES

1 Castle Pines Village, promotional portfolio, 1993. Collection of the Suburban Documentation Project, Minneapolis.

2 Timothy Egan, "House of a Different Color is Shunned," *New York Times* (7 June 1993, Midwest Edition).

3 Karrie Jacobs, "Beep!," *Metropolis* (Dec. 1993), 34-53.

4 Jacobs, "Beep!," 51.

5 As Yi-Fu Tuan has argued, the new wilderness is the city and, for our purposes, we can say that its dangers have been no less mythologized than those of the frontier that faced colonial settlers.

6 David Guterson, "No Place Like Home: On the Manicured Streets of a Master-Planned Community," *Harpers* (November 1992), 55-65.

7 Guterson, "No Place Like Home," 65.

8 Timothy Egan, "House of a Different Color is Shunned."

9 Glen Oaks, promotional portfolio, 1993. Collection of the Suburban Documentation Project.

10 Glen Oaks, promotional portfolio, 1993.

11 Glen Oaks, promotional portfolio, 1993.

12 Castle Pines, promotional portfolio, 1993.

13 Bearpath, promotional portfolio, 1994. Collection of the Suburban Documentation Project.

14 Bearpath, promotional portfolio, 1994.

15 Bearpath, promotional portfolio, 1994.

16 Bearpath, promotional portfolio, 1994.

17 Glen Oaks, promotional portfolio, 1994.

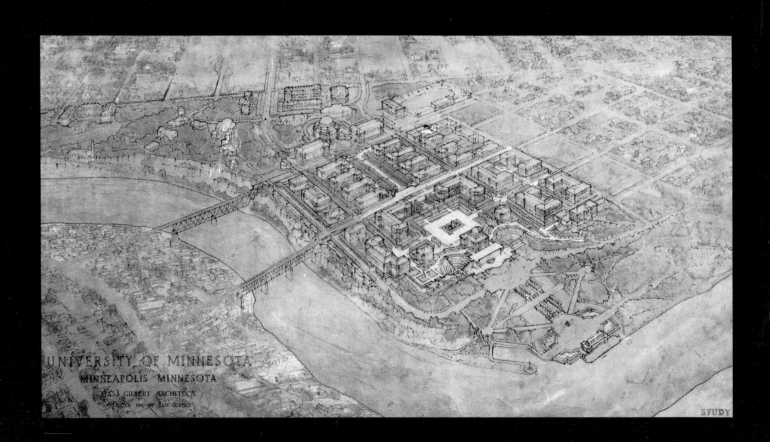

UNIVERSITY OF MINNESOTA
MINNEAPOLIS MINNESOTA
CASS GILBERT ARCHITECT
COPYRIGHTED 1910 BY CASS GILBERT

STUDY

ON CAMPUS PLANNING

MICHAEL DENNIS

The following observations are not those of a campus planning expert; rather, they are based on the author's research and experience as an architect and teacher involved with campus design and planning issues. The focus here is on the physical design of the environment and the conventions that produce it. This seems especially important now, since most campuses have suffered considerably from recent building and yet are poised on the edge of major new building initiatives within their finite boundaries. Worse still, many will leap with no vision, no plan, and no process.

Michael Dennis is a principal of Michael Dennis and Associates in Boston, Massachusetts and is Professor of Architecture at Massachusetts Institute of Technology.

Rendering of Master Plan, University of Minnesota, Cass Gilbert, 1910.

Despite the Elysian connotations of the word *campus*, American universities have until recently been among our most original and poignant models of urban form. Joseph-Jacques Ramée's Union College and Thomas Jefferson's Academical Village provided an enlightened direction in the early nineteenth century. Like physical mirrors of the American Constitution, these campuses projected an image of balanced reciprocity between the public and private realms, between the ideal and the circumstantial. This campus planning tradition, carried through the land grant colleges of the nineteenth century and the educational wing of the City Beautiful movement in the twentieth century, served us well. It was even able to absorb and accommodate the large and functionally complex modern building programs, such as libraries, science buildings, and physical education buildings, that were introduced in the first half of the twentieth century.

Within the last fifty years, however, that campus planning tradition has been almost entirely abandoned, with disastrous results. Since the Second World War, the continued decline of the physical environment through bad planning, bad building, and bad landscaping has exacted a heavy toll. This is not to say that all modern buildings are bad—they are not,

1. *The University of Notre Dame*, engraving, c. 1888.

nor are all traditional buildings good. It is simply that we have produced an embarrassingly greater proportion of bad buildings and places in our time. There are three important and interrelated reasons for this: the anti-urban characteristics of modern architecture, the demise of the master plan, and the emphasis on process.

Modern architecture began to appear sporadically on our campuses in the 1940s, and it rapidly became the norm in a burst of expansive optimism after the Second World War. Modernism offered a vision of progress, promise, and newness. Any campus with money could project an entirely new image—an image of the future, without nostalgia. Unfortunately, novelty is difficult to sustain over time, and Disney's Tomorrowland quickly becomes passé. Indeed, we could easily be convinced that many of our campuses had at one time hosted a world's fair, given their sad collection of what appear to be theme pavilions.

Thus, most campuses now have two codes or sets of conventions: *traditional* and *modern*.

TRADITIONAL VERSUS MODERN PLANNING

Traditionally, buildings and landscape cooperated to define and shape the space of the public realm. The façade of the building was especially important as it was the enclosing wall of the public space. It articulated the public realm, distinguishing it from the private realm inside, and enabled traditional buildings to be quite fat, or deep, without appearing to be so. Landscape elements such as trees and hedges further reinforced and enriched the relationship of building to civic space. Block buildings or courtyard buildings also offered an almost endless array of typological variants.

In contrast, modern buildings, with their irregular shapes, appear to have been generated from the inside out, with no regard for the external environment. They have no façades, only skins or envelopes, and they usually sit in the middle of their sites, so they always seem to be presenting their backsides. Providing some continuous matrix for these suburban buildings requires

2. Memorial Gymnasium, University of Virginia, before 1950.

landscaping that is both picturesque and profuse. Finally, because they are frequently tall elevator buildings and because they withdraw from their site edges, modern buildings often appear larger than their traditional counterparts, even when they are not. Thus we have the duality of the "conversations" of traditional buildings, which speak to each other and together define the public realm, versus the "interior monologues" of modern buildings.

This distinction between traditional and modern is especially important as campuses become more dense and impacted—as they become more literally urban. The civic responsibilities of both buildings and people increase exponentially as they come into closer proximity. A rural campus with widely spaced buildings, such as the University of California at Santa Barbara, may achieve almost complete independence of buildings, but in so doing it becomes more like a summer camp or a resort than an academic community. To be a community requires density and proximity; that is, it requires urbanity.

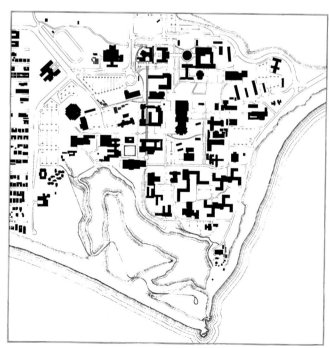

3. Campus Plan, The University of California at Santa Barbara, 1983.

5. Recreational athletics building and dormitories, University of Southern California, 1993.

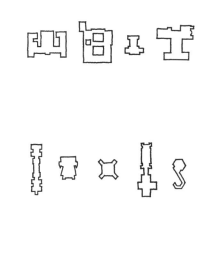

5. Plan diagram of traditional and modern building types at the University of Southern California.

The most successful American campuses have this quality of urbanity. They are generally of two types: those where the campus is like a city, such as Cornell University or the University of Virginia, and those where the campus is—or was—literally a continuous part of the city fabric, such as the University of Southern California or Virginia Commonwealth University. The great Midwestern campuses, such as the University of Minnesota, and the University of Illinois, may be combinations of both. In this regard the importance of Jefferson's plan for the University of Virginia cannot be ignored.

LESSONS OF THE LAWN

It is no accident that Jefferson referred to his plan as an "academical village," for it is a metaphor of society and of the city—a neoclassical ideal adapted to the circumstances of the place. Like the American Constitution, it is an elegantly balanced debate between public and private interests.

For almost two hundred years Jefferson's University has been the most compelling image of American social, political, and academic ideals. The delineation of his idea is so strong and clear that its physical manifestation transcends time to touch each new generation in a fresh and profound way. If today it seems less academically practical than in Jefferson's time, its continuing success should only reinforce our conviction that a true plan for the future must provide for the ideal as well as the circumstantial. Without the civilizing presence of the ideal, circumstance and practicality have no meaning. The Lawn might therefore serve as both a useful model and as a critique of other campuses; especially of successive parts of the University of Virginia's "Grounds."

The formal concept of the Lawn is, in fact, quite simple. As in the traditional city, the clarity and stability of the central public square and the clear pattern of the public streets allow, indeed promote, variation in the form of private pavilions and gardens.

6. The Lawn at the University of Virginia.

Leon Krier has said that a clear center is a necessity, but clear edges are a luxury. If that is true, Jefferson's academical village is truly luxurious, for at least three of its edges are also clear. The two outer ranges define a public street to the west and the crest of the hill to the east, while the rotunda forms a picturesque public face to the north. Only the south side, originally open to the landscape but now closed by a building, remains ambiguous.

The point is that campus design is urban design, and urban design is the design and management of the public realm; of public spaces more than the private realm of individual buildings. The most important lesson of the Lawn for campus planning is that precise control of public space allows for flexibility and change in individual buildings, and it should therefore be the principal instrument of physical planning. From Jefferson's time until recently this concept was thoroughly understood.

With the advent of modernism, however, we lost sight of this basic principle. Our campuses, like our cities, have become ever more random accumulations of separate buildings, each serving its own ends but contributing nothing to the whole.

Imagine the University of Virginia without the Lawn, for example, or with modern "practical" buildings and plenty of parking in its place. Such a plan would resemble countless other nondescript American campuses where well-programmed (though bland) buildings have been randomly distributed between underground utility lines; the only continuity being provided by the landscape.

LESSONS OF THE PLAN

Jefferson's plan was consistently completed after his death, but limited campus development during the nineteenth-century prevented it from exerting much influence until the end of the century. Between 1890 and 1915, small, sometimes heterogeneous colleges began the transition to large, complex modern universities, and many new universities were founded. These changes required a vision, a plan, and a process, which were provided by the American extension of the French *Beaux-Arts* system, the City Beautiful movement.

The instruments that guided the formation of these campuses were usually a plan, which described the physical layout; an aerial perspective, which described the intended character and three-dimensional development; and a president, or university governing body who interpreted the plan and image. In other words, there were campus designs—designs represented by a plan and an image that were intended to guide development either by consistent completion or by re-interpretation.

Most of these designs were highly unified compositions, and even though people at the time realized the improbability of exact completion, the designs at least served as a guide for their decisions. One example of a highly unified design during this period was Henry Hornbostel's re-interpretation of Jefferson's plan in the competition-winning entry for Carnegie Institute of Technology (now Carnegie Mellon University) in 1904. Hornbostel's plan was developed with reasonable consistency until after the Second World War. Another, more city-like,

example was Cass Gilbert's spectacular 1910 plan for the University of Minnesota, a large portion of which was carried out. Both campuses suffered greatly from thoughtless postwar additions, but the strength of their cores allowed them to survive later mutilations; just as Jefferson's Lawn still deflects attention from a continuing succession of inept modern additions to the rest of the University.

Most of these campuses benefited not just from one plan, but from a series of plans. The University of Illinois, for example, had at least thirteen plans in the nine years between 1905 and 1914. The official *Plan for the Development of the Campus,* by Charles A. Platt, was adopted in 1922 and revised in 1927. Far from being absolute, these early campus plans were part of a continuously evolving process of development.

As an instrument of traditional planning the campus plan fell into disrepute following the Second World War. In the postwar period the campus plan became known as the master plan, with all the expectations of certitude the name implies. Unlike its predecessor, however, the master plan was too often taken literally rather than as an instrument of speculation and re-interpretation. Since the master plan appeared finite and inca-

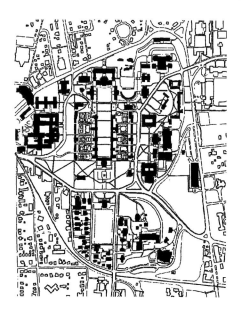
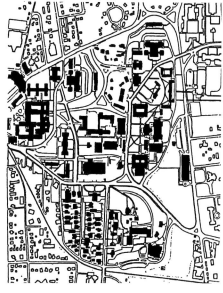

7. Plan of Central Grounds, University of Virginia.

8. Hypothetical Plan of Central Grounds without the Lawn.

9. Rendering of Master Plan,
Carnegie Institute of Technology,
Henry Hornbostel, 1906.

pable of change, and since it was frequently a legal document, it could never be current enough to guide the dynamic unpredictability of the evolving modern campus. That it could have provided a vision, and implicit guidelines, was lost to the modernist minds of administrators, architects, and planners, pressured by expedience and by rapid expansion in a time of increasingly participatory campus governance.

The modernist answer was, of course, *process*. Since most master plans were out of date even before they were completed and approved, what was needed apparently was a rational decision-making process; one that would substitute the deliberations of a democratic bureaucracy for unilateral decisions based on often capricious taste and judgment. The great irony is, of course, that an elegant process is the result of ideas and goals, informed by taste and judgement, and rarely emerges from bureaucratic considerations. Consequently, what happened more often than not was the politics of power rather than process. The results are around us everywhere, yet nobody ever seems responsible for

them. Either they "were not in the room when it happened" or "it was already too late" or it was "not their department" or it was "a result of the budget and schedule."

If traditional campus planning conventions are like those of urban design, modern campus planning conventions are more like those of homesteading. Despite the seductive urban implications of campuses, they may have suffered more than cities from the demise of conventions and consensus precisely because they are not like cities in one fundamental way: a city is composed of connected public spaces and smaller private plots. Much of this form is governed by laws and codes. Campuses make no such distinctions. There are usually no laws, and property lines exist only in the imaginations of deans. Campuses, even state ones, are more like courts, such as that of Louis at Versailles, where favors are obtained in curious ways and even tenure does not guarantee authority. Campus design is therefore subject not only to the power of deans and the unpredictability of funding by donors, but often to the imposition of their tastes as well. This was difficult

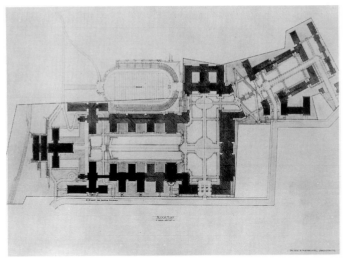

10. Plan, Carnegie Institute of Technology, Henry Hornbostel, 1906.

11. Aerial View of Hornbostel Mall, Carnegie Mellon University.

enough when taste and judgement were embedded in convention. Now the problem is infinitely worse. As our campuses are becoming more and more dense, the conventions of homesteading have become obsolete, useless, and undesirable. We are now faced with the task of developing a modern architecture that acknowledges, and is compatible with, traditional environments. This requires a planning strategy that promotes the civic responsibilities of individual buildings.

COMPREHENSIVE DESIGN AND PLANNING

By now it should be apparent that there is not an easy answer to producing a coherent campus environment. Minimally, three things are required: a *vision*, a *plan*, and a *process*. Another requirement is to choose architects very, very carefully. No vision, plan, or process offers protection from a bad architect. Conversely, a good architect will not be repressed by a clear vision, a well thought-out plan, and an intelligent process. Good architects can even provide these things, but it is more logical for a university to suggest and continuously monitor its own identity.

Vision   A vision for the modern campus can be elusive and difficult to articulate, especially as it varies from campus to campus. There are two important ideas that underlie any vision: that the physical environment matters; and that there is a relationship between academic ideals and physical reality.

A university is not a summer camp or a resort, although on occasion our typical campus may appear so to the European eye, accustomed as it is to another mode. Nor is a university a city. Some campuses may form part of one, and others would be large enough to qualify if size were the only criteria. Rather, a university is quasi-urban. Like a model for the city it is at once more ideal and more practical; a textbook of *civitas*. It is therefore not enough for a university to have an intellectual vision: that vision must also bear a relationship to society as a whole, and the campus should mirror that idea. Thus, campus design is urban design, and it must balance the public interests of the larger environment and the private interests of users and donors. Accomplishing this requires both a plan and a process.

Plans and Guidelines   Three levels of plans and guidelines are required before the design of individual buildings can begin: a campus plan, precinct plans, and site plans. The campus plan establishes the overall intent of the university. It defines the primary spatial anatomy, the hierarchical pattern of public spaces of the campus, as well as its relationship to its surroundings. As such it should be a design plan that suggests the quality of buildings and spaces, not a generic plan as in a use and circulation diagram. The campus plan should also be accompanied by general design principles that apply to the whole campus, and by specific design guidelines that apply to the primary public spaces.

The precinct plan is, in practice, the most effective tool for managing campus development. As a "neighborhood" plan it

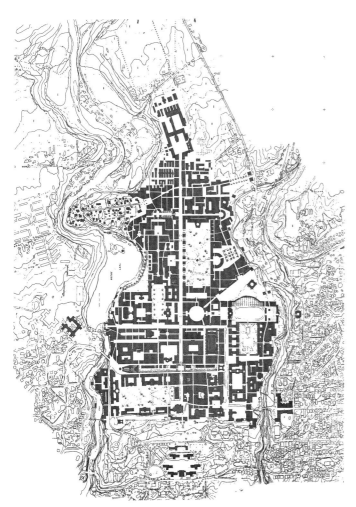

12. **Campus Plan, Cornell University, 1981.**

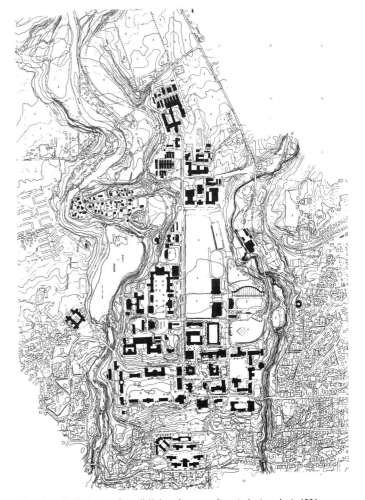

13. **Hypothetical plan, Cornell University as a city, student project, 1981.**

bridges the gap between the campus plan (traditionally the master plan) and the siting and design of individual buildings. The precinct plan adds flexibility and precision to the campus plan and saves it from having to be specific about everything. A precinct plan should also be accompanied by specific design guidelines regarding the form of public open space and the architectural character of buildings.

The site plan is really the result of feasibility studies that determine the conceptual, economic, and environmental impact of a given building program. The site plan conveys to the architect more specific requirements not covered by the precinct plan and should be accompanied by guidelines unique to the particular building.

Together these three types of plans and guidelines are the tools or instruments of campus development. They are an indispensable part of the process.

Process   To be effective, any process must address both private and public interests. In the recent past this balance has been difficult to achieve due to the hegemony of private interests resulting from the lack of both vision and design authority. Maintaining a balance requires the active participation and cooperation of four entities: the users, the physical plant, the design authority, and the architect. Each must be involved with all phases and accept responsibility for the implications and effects of their individual agendas. For example, it is not enough for a design authority to make requirements in the early design phases of a project and then be absent in the later phases when budget considerations threaten to undermine those requirements. Most importantly, everyone involved must agree not to knowingly make questionable decisions for the sake of expediency. There can be no excuse for making things badly: not schedule, not budget, not process.

The users have a largely private agenda. They are primarily concerned with getting the most floor area possible and the best functional arrangement. Every user group's special requirements must be acknowledged, but its needs must also be put in the larger context; the financial, formal, and social program. For example, to fulfill the facility's responsibilities to the public realm, the exterior of the building and the site development should be subject to appropriate budgetary attention.

The physical plant, or facilities management group, also typically has a largely private agenda as it is concerned primarily with budget and schedule. To the degree that it is also a planning authority it may also be concerned with the long-term viability of the project, its engineering, and its maintenance. In this last sense, it may also have a public agenda.

The design authority of a university, in contrast to the users and the physical plant, has an almost completely public agenda. Though the design authority, like the physical plant, is interested in the long-term viability of a project, its primary concerns are the promotion, development, and maintenance of the quality of the public realm. Thus, it plays a large role in the development of plans and guidelines, in architect selection, and in the design review of individual projects. A design authority may be an individual, a group of individuals, or a design review committee. Its power or authority, and therefore its effectiveness, may be delegated from the top down or developed from the bottom up. Both are desirable, but without support from the top the effectiveness of consensus is drastically diminished. Design review, long the domain of the user and the physical plant, should be extended to the design authority or committee. After an initial meeting to clarify the university's intent, there should be formal intermediate and final reviews of the schematic design and design development phases of all projects; and, if there are significant changes, there should be equivalent reviews for construction documents. A post-construction assessment should also be done by the design authority.

The architect alone must have an acutely developed understanding of both public and private obligations. This is frequently a problem, since architects in our time have become very adept at servicing and delivering complex programs, but less skilled at designing the public realm. Specialists in a particular building type have an understandable appeal to users of that building type, and yet such firms may have no credentials at all for design in the environment in which the facility is placed. Indeed, specialist firms are too often merely poor to mediocre firms with good marketing departments. Creating associations or teams may be one way to solve this problem: selecting a good design firm and requiring them to have a specialist as a consultant, rather than the reverse. In any case, the design authority should play a central role in architect selection and design review. Finally, each architect should be required to show his or her project "in context" using area plans, models, and perspectives.

If we are to regain the successes of our earlier campus traditions, we must find a new way of planning and guiding the campus development process. The result will not be completely unified campuses, nor should it. Most campuses are now already heterogeneous, but it should produce a new order, one that promotes rather than prevents community and fosters a high-quality physical environment. That environment will necessarily be more urban. Beyond that, we can only hope it will promote the kind of dialogue we associate with the best American academic and civic ideals.

THEORY AND PRACTICE

In recent years both practice and academia have provided fertile ground for campus design research. The design studio has allowed for the willing suspension of disbelief and therefore odd but provocative investigation that would not be well received by paying clients. Two recent studio projects, for Cornell University and Carnegie Mellon University, explored the idea of making an existing campus plan as dense as possible, as if it were a city, in order to render more visible the presence of a delicate but elusive urban structure. Strangely, the exaggeration of urban density made it possible to imagine an intermediate design condition: one

between campus and city that was at once urban and Elysian. It also identified strategic sites where one building or complex could firmly indicate a new pattern of development or reinforce an existing one. This last point is crucial because as an architect one often gets only one building to design. If that building is to be more than just another homestead, it should be imagined as a fragment of a larger plan. In other words, each new building must produce its own master plan or re-interpretation of a master plan.

The language or style of each new building should also be considered in a similar way to the form or type. Donors usually want their legacy to be unique—to be a monument or a "signature" building—but few campus buildings merit such complete and autonomous distinction. Rather, it is possible for buildings to have their own identity, while also relating to the continuity of the place and becoming part of the campus fabric.

Over the last few years our office has explored these campus design issues in both competitions and commissions. From fragmentary additions, such as the Music Building Expansion at Arizona State University, to precinct plans for Syracuse University, the University of Virginia, and the University of Southern California, and to the extensive campus design plan for Carnegie Mellon University, we have pursued, transformed, and adapted these principles to circumstances of the place.

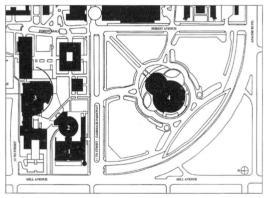

ARIZONA STATE UNIVERSITY

Located at the formal entry to the Arizona State University campus, the new Music Building joins an ensemble of three monumental public buildings, each of which has a unique form and architectural character: the Gammage Center, by Frank Lloyd Wright; the Fine Arts Center, by Antoine Predock; and the existing Music Building, by the Taliesin Fellowship.

In contrast to the complex massing of the Fine Arts Center, the new building presents a simple and straightforward overall form, which reinforces the streets that adjoin it and marks the corner. It is intended to strengthen the urban spatial order of the area, providing a counterpoint to its freestanding neighbors.

The exterior surfaces are simple abstract stucco planes, colored a violet shade of desert rose that relates to both the gray-violet of the Fine Arts Center and the desert rose of the Music Building and the Gammage Center. Openings in the exterior wall are small, but in the courtyard and garden large areas of glass, shaded by planting and trellises, open the inside public space to the outside. The south-facing wing along Gammage Parkway contains an open loggia, which provides a shady pedestrian route along the street and into the building. At the center of the loggia an open passage connects to a paved courtyard. Beyond the courtyard lies a new double-height lobby, linking the addition to the existing building while framing views.

14. Music Building expansion.
15. Arts precinct plan.
16. Music Building expansion.

SYRACUSE UNIVERSITY

This precinct plan includes a studio art building and a science/technology center to be built in phases, beginning with a large multidisciplinary building devoted to computer science and chemistry. The key elements of the plan are an extended tree-lined terrace along College Place and a court formed along the central axis of the campus quadrangle. The terrace, planted with a double row of deciduous trees, overlooks the historic campus to the west from a slightly raised elevation. The primary facades of the new science buildings will be along this terrace. In the middle of the terrace is the central space of the new development. Lined with evergreen trees, this court opens to the great facade of Slocum Hall across the street.

The science building is organized around this court and along the terrace. The height of the new building, the materials, and the base and cornice lines relate directly to the traditional campus buildings across College Place to create a unified street. As in the main campus, the principal materials are brick and stone. The chemistry wing is developed as a large pilastered wall on a base—like a great colonnade or loggia. Future buildings along the terrace should have a similar, if not identical, character.

Adjacent to one of the heavily traveled pedestrian routes on the campus, the Art Building is located at a physical, functional, and symbolic hub at the corner of the main quadrangle. It thus forms a gateway to the science/technology center, bringing art and science into daily juxtaposition.

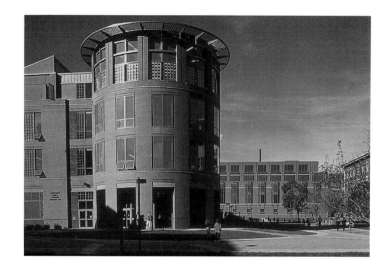

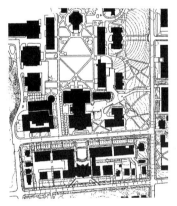

17. View from the main quadrangle showing the Art Building and the Science/Technology Building beyond.

18. Main quadrangle and Hendricks Chapel.

19. Proposed precinct plan.

20. Model view of the Science/Technology Building courtyard.

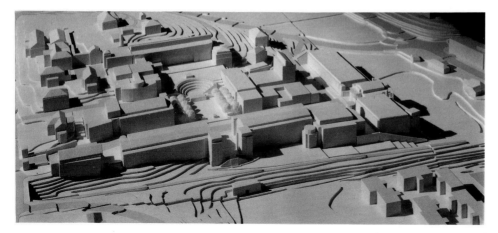

UNIVERSITY OF VIRGINIA

The crest of Carr's Hill is occupied by the University of Virginia president's house, which faces south toward Thomas Jefferson's "Academical Village," the core of the university. The eastern boundary of this precinct, Rugby Road, is lined by small brick buildings that are, like the president's house, of traditional architectural character. Cut into the north side of the hill, by contrast, are modern buildings dedicated to architecture and drama; the remnants of an unrealized courtyard plan.

The University envisions an "Acropolis of the Arts" on Carr's Hill. The new plan includes major additions to the architecture, art history, drama, buildings as well as the fine arts library, and new facilities to accommodate music concerts, music education, TV/film, dance, studio art, and an art museum. Also included is structured parking for 800 cars.

The formal strategy for accomplishing this task is to complete the implied organization of the existing buildings by clearly defining a central square and by connecting it to Rugby Road with a new street. Thus, the dense core of the precinct is enveloped by small existing buildings preserved on two sides. The remaining two sides are lined with new monumental buildings, providing the University with prominent facades that signal entrance to the grounds. The project is designed to be built in phases and to be coherent at each stage.

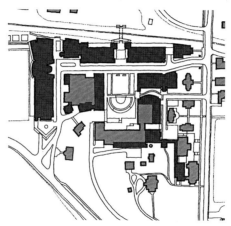

21. Model view.
22. View towards the Drama building.
23. Plan for an "Acropolis of the Arts".
24. View towards Lambeth field.

UNIVERSITY OF SOUTHERN CALIFORNIA

The University of Southern California is a relatively dense urban campus that has evolved within the street pattern of downtown Los Angeles. The traditional buildings that form the core of the campus relate directly to this street pattern; most of the numerous modern buildings do not.

The goal of this precinct plan is to reorganize the public open space and provide for future buildings in two quadrants of the USC campus. The impetus for the project was the construction of a new library and the desire to remove an existing diagonal street, Hoover Boulevard. Gradually, Hoover Boulevard has become an isolated remnant of the city grid, internal to the campus and no longer connected to the surrounding fabric. Removing it enables the campus to recoup a large open space and to reintegrate the previously separated triangular area.

The design presents a series of new quadrangles, the largest of which unites the old and new libraries and, more generally, serves as a forum to the area. The "town & gown" area also capitalizes on the removal of Hoover Boulevard to reorganize the public open space, identify significant future building sites, and make a major new formal entrance to the campus. This area offers unique opportunities for architectural expression. Located across the street from Exposition Park and a new subway stop, it terminates the palm-lined diagonal of Figueroa Street. Thus, it is geographically and symbolically the most important corner of the campus.

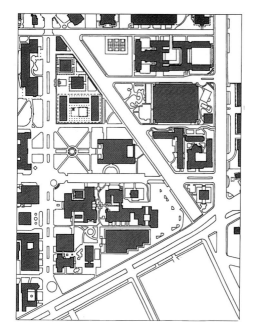 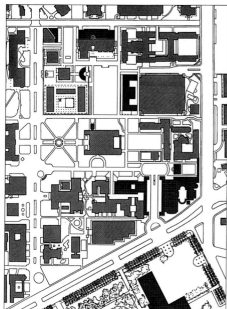

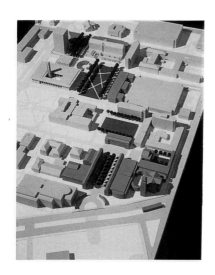

25. Plan of the Library and "Town & Gown" precincts.
26. Proposed plan for the Library and "Town & Gown" precincts.
27. Perspective view of proposed Library Quadrangle.
28. Model view of the proposed plan.

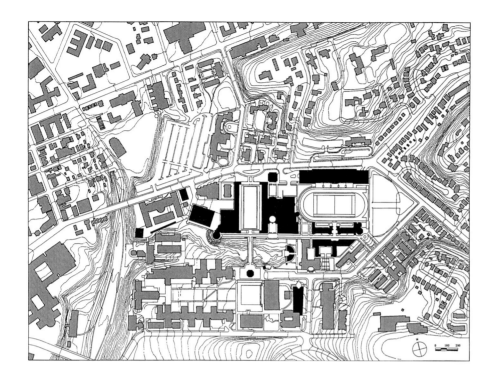

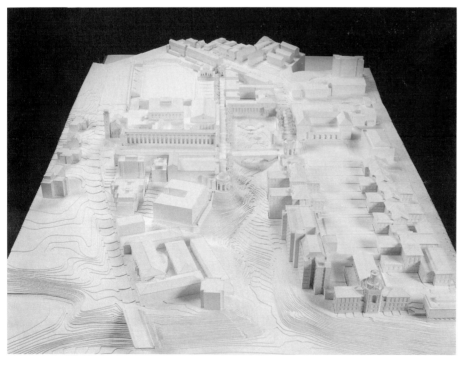

CARNEGIE MELLON UNIVERSITY

Henry Hornbostel's 1904 competition-winning plan for what is now Carnegie Mellon University was never completed. Although the core of his plan—he mall—is nominally complete, it has suffered considerably from numerous insensitive modern additions—buildings that are stylistically and/or typologically incompatible with his work.

In the spring of 1987 the University held a competition for a new campus plan. Included in the program were a University Center, Performing Arts Center, Dormitory/Dining Hall, varsity athletic field with running track, tennis courts, and a new pedestrian street, as well as proposals for future buildings

This project, the winning design, centers on the idea of the "urbanization" of the campus through density of development and the definition of the public domain. Specifically, a measured and varied sequence of new outdoor spaces is designed to relate to and complete Hornbostel's original quadrangle. A central feature of the new composition is the romantic landscape—the ravine—that rises from Panther Hollow to a new amphitheater in front of Margaret Morrison Hall. There had previously been a valley in the same location, but it was partially filled some years ago. This reconstructed landscape both unites and articulates the old and new parts of the campus and allows the new pedestrian street to function as a south-facing terrace overlooking the ravine.

An articulate public space network for the campus has two primary benefits. It promotes flexibility; being sufficiently specific in its own right, it can accommodate numerous building interpretations and revisions over time. It also serves as a social armature for student, faculty, and public interaction, as well as a formal instrument of campus identity and university life.

Each individual building contributes to the public structure in some way, but each is also free to adapt to its own internal requirements. Large buildings, such as the University Center, are articulated into smaller idealized components that break down the scale and increase planning flexibility.

After the competition, the program for the eastern portion of the campus was expanded to include intramural fields and parking while the program for the University Center was reduced. This necessitated a revised campus design plan, which was approved in 1988.

The first phase of the revised plan, the East Campus Project, includes a dormitory for 300 students, a 400-seat dining hall, a 600-car parking structure, varsity and intramural athletic fields, and a pedestrian street and plaza. The Dormitory and Parking Garage enclose a football field and running track, thus forming a new athletic quadrangle. The second phase, the University Center, closes the athletic quadrangle, extends the pedestrian street, and defines the eastern edge of the formal quadrangle known as the Cut. The third phase, the Center for the Arts, completes the core of the composition by defining the western edge of the Cut and terminating the pedestrian street. The fourth phase of the project is envisioned as landscape development, especially of the ravine, and as an opportunity to develop further buildings.

Finally, an Electronic Materials Technology Building is proposed on one of the most prominent sites on the campus. Since 1914 Hornbostel's Machinery Hall (now Hamerschlag Hall) has been the most important physical image of Carnegie Mellon University. On top of a steep slope, overlooking Panther Hollow and the Carnegie Museum, the building is at once the terminal element of the Hornbostel Mall within the campus and the visual symbol of the university to the public realm beyond. Thus, any addition or expansion to the west must not obscure the building but enhance both it and the context.

The idea is to provide a much needed base for Hornbostel's building so that the two distinct parts form a unified ensemble reminiscent of Hornbostel's first scheme for the site. Like our other designs for the campus, this project is designed with the scale, degree of detail, and spirit of the existing Hornbostel buildings. The result is a great wall rising from the valley floor to complete Hornbostel's composition.

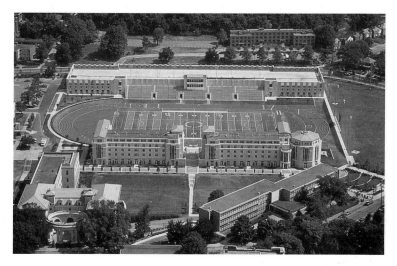

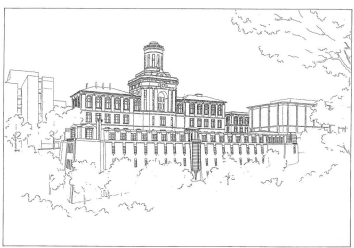

Opposite

29. Proposed Campus plan.

30. Model view of competition scheme.

Right

31. Preliminary study for the Center for the Arts.

32. Aerial view of East Campus Project, showing the dormitory, athletic field and parking garage/stadium.

33. Preliminary study for the Electronic Materials Technology Building.

FIGURE CREDITS

1 Courtesy University of Minnesota.
2 Courtesy University of Notre Dame.
3,6 Prints File, University Archives, Special Collections, University of Virginia.
9,10 Courtesy Carnegie Mellon University
20 Photo by William T. Smith
32,34 ©Jeff Goldberg/Esto.

All other figures courtesy of the Author.

PROJECT CREDITS

Arizona State University
Music Building Expansion
Design Architect: Michael Dennis, Jeffrey Clark & Associates.
Architect: DWL/ The Mathes Group.

Syracuse University
Precinct Plan
Architect: Koetter, Kim & Associates and Michael Dennis, Jeffrey Clark & Associates.

Science/ Technology Building
Design Architect: Koetter, Kim & Associates and Michael Dennis, Jeffrey Clark & Associates.
Architect: The Kling-Lindquist Partnership, Inc.

Shaffer Art Building
Conceptual Design: Koetter, Kim & Associates and Michael, Jeffrey Clark & Associates.
Design Architect: Koetter, Kim & Associates.
Architect: Fugligni-Fragola/Architects.

University of Virginia
Carr's Hill Precinct Plan
Architect: Michael Dennis & Associates.

Carnegie Mellon University
Campus Plan
Architect: Michael Dennis, Jeffrey Clark & Associates.

East Campus Project
Design Architect: Michael Dennis, Jeffrey Clark & Associates.
Architect: TAMS Consultants, Inc.

University Center
Conceptual Design: Michael Dennis, Jeffrey Clark & Associates.
Architect: UDA/MDA Architects, a joint-venture of UDA Architects and Michael Dennis & Associates.

Center for the Arts
Preliminary Design Study: Michael Dennis & Associates.

Electronic Materials Technology Building
Preliminary Design Study: Michael Dennis & Associates.

34. Carnegie Mellon. View of the athletic field and stadium from the dormitory.

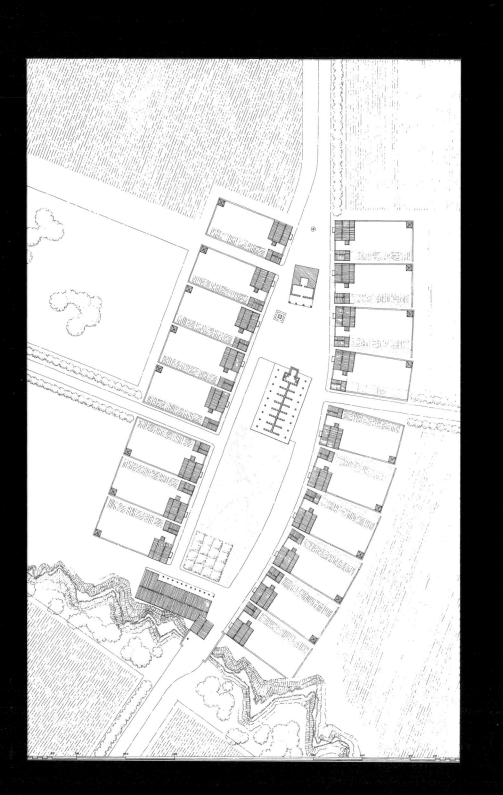

THE VILLAGE OF WASHINGTON RIDGE

ANNE MUNLY + B. T. LESLIE

Anne Munly is Assistant Professor of Architecture at Syracuse University where she teaches design and analysis of American Urbanism.

b. t. leslie is Associate Professor at Syracuse University and is partner in the firm Munly/Brown Architects.

In 1987 a competition for a single family house was sponsored by The Washington Ridge Conservancy and Ms. Anne Dalton in order to establish design standards for 22 rural 'villa' lots to be developed on a 162 acre tract in rural Litchfield County, Connecticut. The competition brief encouraged "the creative interpretation of the rural domestic architecture found in New England," which honors "the spatial character of the classic New England farmhouse: a system of interconnected masses, with materials and proportions inspired by the region's eighteenth and nineteenth century buildings." Rejecting the proposed agricultural idiom as antithetical to the aims of a civil oriented development, we based our design on the urban traditions of the New England small town. The following observations/convictions influenced the development of our scheme.

Suburban expansion, at any scale, upsets the symbiotic relationship between the natural landscape, or agricultural land, and the urban environment, a relationship of mutual dependence, rather than mutual destruction. The subdivision of the land proposed by the competition increases infrastructure costs and isolates the individual or family from the political and civic activity associated with city life. In contrast, the New England agricultural community is traditionally centered on the village, not on the individuated farm house. The inspiration for our scheme rests in the New England small town, not in the agrarian tradition.

Self-sufficiency is paramount to the growth and ultimate legitimacy of any town. The historical development of the self-sufficient community indicates a disposition of private and public building within a hierarchic urban structure through which growth may occur. Early New England towns exhibit a compactness which supports the participation of the individual in the political and social life of the town, as all the components necessary for daily life are included within close proximity.

Site Plan.

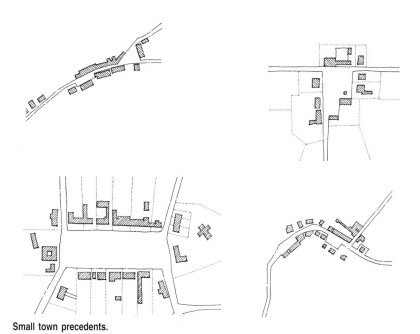

Small town precedents.

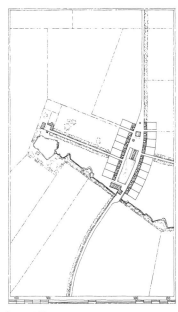

Context Plan.

Critical to the proposal for the Village of Washington Ridge is the inclusion of the public realm in the development of the village. The integration of residential and institutional components fosters the growth of a self-sufficient community. The aim of the proposal is to create a legitimate small town or village, not to be misconstrued as a village-like suburban development. Consequently, the project anticipates an alternative life-style to that of the suburban commuter and challenges the typical displacement of the residential component of the city into the suburban landscape.

Our proposed village is sited at a crossroads near the juncture of a riverbed and the main road, with houses organized around a town green at a widening of the road. The competition site encompassed one 3 1/2 acre parcel, of which only 3/4 acre was to be developed as the villa proper; the model home for the subsequent 22 individual villas. Our counter-proposal calls for the use of approximately 20 acres for the town, leaving 140 acres for cultivation and future expansion.

We looked to the precedents of the town green, the meeting

hall, and the market of the New England Village as the rudiments for the establishment of *place* at the crossroads, so as to provide the nucleus for future growth and development of the village. The most important of these structures is the Meeting Hall/ Market, belonging to a typology of buildings with public rooms placed above an open market hall. Meeting halls played a primary role in the New England community and were often one of the first buildings constructed in a village. Many meeting halls continue to function as the central focus within their community. In our proposal, the Meeting hall/ Market supports the aspiration to self-sufficiency, or at a minimum the political enfranchisement, of the community.

The town green in New England villages, as a component of the public realm, was formally associated with the town hall, meeting hall or other public structures. Its evolution is linked to the historic designation of land within the town to be held in common by the citizens. In our proposal three public buildings occupy the green: the Meeting Hall/ Market in the center of the common; the town gas pump to the north; and the Post Office/

View of town green looking towards Meeting Hall/ Market Building.

General Store to the south.   In our project, the town green is provided to support the development of the civic life of the town and the civic participation of the individual.

We felt that the housing typology of the village should be the urban house, specifically that found in the New England small town or village. Emphasis on the farmhouse as a repeatable unit, as called for in the competition brief, would have been an exercise in suburban development. Such a pattern undermines the agricultural potential of the land as well as legitimate urban form. We developed a village where the single-family house is one component of the whole . Two house types, one of single-room frontage and the second of double room frontage, are developed, each respecting the street edge. Apartments on the second level of a commercial building introduce a third type of dwelling unit.

The Village of Washington Ridge should be understood as an alternative settlement, not meant to challenge the primacy of the city, but rather to complement it.

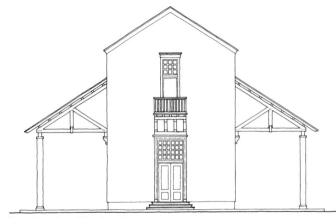

Front elevation of Meeting Hall.

Village house type.

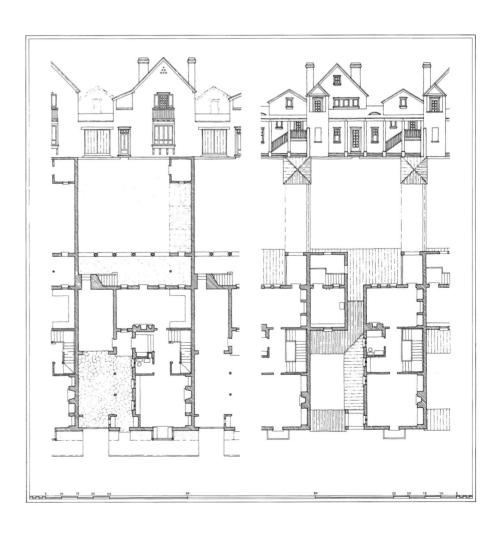

Variation of house type .

View of green looking towards Post Office/ General Store.

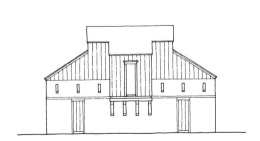

Elevation of Bath House.

Study for Post Office/ General Store.

FIGURE CREDITS

All drawings courtesy of the author.
Project received Honorable Mention.

VIOLENCE, MATERIALISM AND RITUAL: SHOPPING FOR A CENTER

JONATHAN F. P. ROSE

I am an environmental planner and a real estate developer. My work is to build communities, or pieces of them. I hope to make villages, towns and cities viable, and by doing so, to preserve the land around them.

Jonathan F. P. Rose is President of Affordable Housing Construction Corp. in Katonah, New York.

With the decline of many American cities has come an alarming increase in suburbanization, which is consuming agricultural land, forest land, and wilderness at an astounding rate. How can we change this entropic pattern of settlement so that development reflects the self balancing qualities of organic systems?[1] What must we learn so that our communities are economically, socially, and environmentally healthy—in short, sustainable?

I suggest that we begin by looking at the life cycles of cities in many times and in many different cultures. We often see that cities rise with great bursts of community-building energy and commitment to the common good but then decline in a morass of violence, individualism, and materialism. Numerous symptoms of disconnection of the individual from place and culture are evident in America today; much as organic systems flower above the desert of entropy, ultimately to wither when they are no longer able to sustain their order. Just as organic systems either grow, decay or stabilize in health cycles, cities also follow these patterns.

It is hard to discern whether the cultural changes we see when cities decline are the causes of decline or merely symptoms of decline. Cities seem to decline when they develop a self-indulgent (materialistic) rather than a civic culture—perhaps when their size sprawls beyond their organizational capacity. Perhaps they decline because of disease and a diseased culture.

As cities descend from their vibrant peaks, violence and death become a public spectacle or sport; whether it be in Roman colosseums, Mayan temples, or in contemporary television and films. Violence often appears in either random or centrally organized patterns. Random violence is a reflection of disconnection, while centrally organized violence such as govern-

E.J. Curtis, *A Feast Day at Acoma*, 1904.

The form of our universe appears to be organized by the rules of thermodynamics. The second law of thermodynamics predicts that energy flows from higher states of organization (complexity) to lower states of organization (stasis). Differentiation of energy states is reflected in form as organization. The ultimate consequence of this flow is that the energy and organization of the universe will equalize (entropy), unless the universe collapses into a new death/birth cycle.

Organic systems have the unique ability to collect energy into structures of increasing organization, in apparent contradiction to the laws of thermodynamics. In fact, this behavior is thermodynamic and is subsidized by an outside energy source. For example, the growth of life on earth is fed by energy from the thermodynamic decay of the sun.

In this sea of entropy, organic systems are able to collect energy, increase their organization and reflect energy and organization as form, information, and even intelligence. Since our own communities are a subset of organic systems, if we can better understand the rules that guide the development of organic systems, and design of our communities to reflect these rules, our own communities may evolve in a more refined way. By studying organic systems we can learn how to channel chaotic changes into cyclical ones and how to use energy, information, and form to counteract decay.[2]

ment-led war or Mayan sacrifice seems to bring societies together in powerful ways. Is violence a way that central governments express their sense of mastery over the unknowable universe? Nonviolent rituals accomplish civic cohesion in a more sustainable manner. Ritual, then, may be a series of symbolic actions connecting us with the unknown in a beneficial way.

If one looks at the relationship between materialism, civic disorder, and violence, one finds at their common root expressions of disconnection from a commitment to the common good. Violence is a psychopathological symptom of one who is unbound from family and society. Those who are woven into their culture feel the pain of the other; this communal empathy is reflected in phrases like "Do unto others as you would have them do unto you," and " Ask not for whom the bell tolls; it tolls for thee." This connection is known as compassion. The person who is centered in himself or herself, and who feels a place in the universe, needs little more than breath, food, and shelter to live contentedly. In traditional cultures, the individual's place is defined by clan, by trade, by a mythology that connects a people to the founding of the universe, and by a community built upon a common understanding of the universe.

Because the contemporary Western built environment is largely determined by economics and not a deeper archetypal mythology, it does not ground us in a place. Our culture gives us little guidance as to who we are; our only roles are as workers and as consumers. The current social contract is based on buying things relentlessly, as though by mastering objects we could master our world. Material consumption is growing at an astounding rate in America. In 1964 we had five square feet of retail space for each American; in 1992, we had eighteen square feet of retail space for each of us.[3] Was this great flowering of K-marts, Wal-Marts and home shopping channels fulfilling an actual need for three times as much stuff in our lives? Is this burgeoning retail the cause or the effect of the undermining of community?

With the rise in consumption, we have seen a rise in violence. Research indicates a correlation between the proportion of single-parent households in a community and the rate of violent crime and burglary in that community. Children from mother-child families are also more susceptible to drug use.[4] Perhaps the teenager, lost among grandmothers, crack mothers, and foster care, is both the cause and the effect of the concomitant inner city violence.

Violence is not just an inner-city phenomenon but a national one. Fourteen children are shot to death each day in America, often in the suburbs and rural areas. There are more gun dealers than gas stations in our country. We manufacture a new gun every 10 seconds, and millions more are imported. Surprisingly, the manufacture of teddy bears

Above: *Human sacrifice.* Codex Magliabecchian, c. 1540.
Below: *Police Verso,* (thumbs down) by Jean-Leon Gerome.

Malidoma Some, a medicine man of the Dagara tribe from Upper Volta (now Burkina Faso), West Africa, writes that for his society, "Initiation is the bridge between youth and adulthood. In my village, a person who is not initiated is considered a child, no matter how old that person is. Without initiation we cannot recall our purpose. To not be initiated is to be a nonperson."

Taken from his village by Jesuit missionaries when he was 4 years old, Malidoma escaped back to his home when he was 20 and asked the elders of the village to allow him to undergo the ritual initiation usually undertaken by 13- and 14-year olds. Malidoma describes the experience as "a six-week journey into the magical world. It begins when families walk their young ones to the outskirts of the village and surrender them to the wilderness. The young ones walk into the bush naked and scared, a condition necessary for the ritual remembering. Throughout the ordeal there is no food except what can be found in the bush."

Malidoma continues, "Early in my initiation I was told to sit in front of a tree and to gaze at it. The hot tropical sun broiled me, ants bit me, and I was blinded by sweat. Every so often an elder would come and check on me. The experience was painful and boring, but it all culminated in a vision in which the tree disappeared and I saw a green woman emerge from it. She was as familiar as a mother or some sacred caretaker. Whoever she was, the reunion was very emotional, and the experience ended with me hugging that tree and weeping."

Malidoma contends that one returns from an initiatory experience equipped "with something that serves as the 'first medicine,' a kind of reference book that you return to whenever you feel the need to refresh your memory of what you are doing here on earth."

On contemporary Western society, Malidoma comments, "Because of the unhappy loss of this kind of initiatory experience, the modern world suffers a kind of spiritual poverty and lack of community. Young people are feared for their wild and dangerous energy, which is really an unending longing for initiation. I think it is urgent that the West quickly learn from indigenous people how to help young people ritualistically focus and transcend their wild energy, demonstrate their worth, and be accepted into a community." [6]

is regulated far more stringently for safety than the manufacture of guns. The movie *Die Hard* featured 264 deaths on screen.[5] Death and violence is, for us, a spectacle; just as it was for earlier Roman, Mayan or Mongolian societies. It is a sign of horrible disconnection.

Disconnection comes from the lack of centering rituals and places in our lives. Traditionally, ritual served to re-connect us to our community, to our place and to the universe. Mircea Eliade eloquently described how a good ritual draws a line through the center of the universe to the center of our being.[7] In indigenous cultures, the hormonal rush that wracks all teenage males is directed by rituals of initiation and becomes an initiation to responsibility and knowledge and place. Without the channeling power of ritual, the adventurous adolescent process of self-definition becomes violent. If one studies homeless people, one learns they often become homeless because of a traumatic event that casts them from their place, such as a fire or violent robbery, and because they lack the skills or resources to reconnect. In interviews, the homeless report their greatest loss is not the loss of objects or even the comfort of shelter, it is their sense of disconnection from community, from a place called home.

If one looks to the history of the rise and fall of cities, one sees that our plague of violence and materialism is common in the cycle of urban life. Before the arrival of cities 5500 years ago, humankind lived in urban and rural villages. Urban villages, dense settlements such as early Jericho, had as many dwellings per acre as future cities would have, but lacked the social and physical diversity that was to flourish when cities later appeared. As one compares these settlements in many cultures, patterns emerge that suggest they were designed by the interaction of three forces—instinct, the environment, and the culture's map of the universe.

Cities arose independently out of seven birthplace cultures, each one undergoing a paradigm shift in which cities emerged suddenly rather than gradually. These first independent civilizations were the Sumerian in Southern Mesopotamia, the Egyptian in the Nile Valley, the Harrapan in the Indus Valley, the Chinese by the Yellow River, the Aztec in the Valley of Mexico, the Maya in the jungles of Guatemala and Honduras, and the Inca on the coastlands and highlands of Peru. The basic form and function of these early cities were remarkably similar. Each were laid out in grids inside defensible walls, had suburbs beyond the walls, and contained streets, temples, storehouses, and palaces. Why do such common forms appear independently on different continents in very different cultures? Could it be that these common elements of form reflect a common genetic code for how to build the kind of place in which human beings are designed to live? If all other animals have an instinct for place making, why shouldn't people?

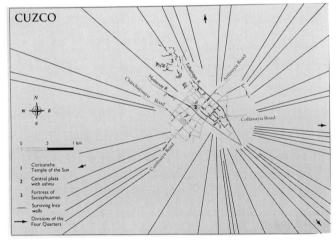

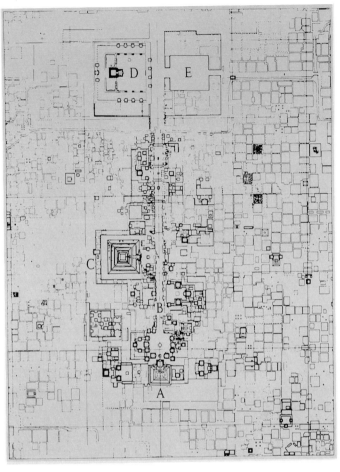

Top: Plaza of Cuzco in Peru.
Middle left: Plan of Teotihuacan
Middle right: Cuzco and the ceque (site line) system, Peru, Inca.
Bottom: The Ritual Way of Teotihuacan.

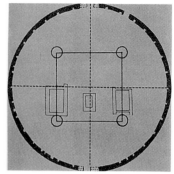

Top left: Kivas. New Mexico, Chaco/Anasazi, Chaco Canyon, Pueble del Arroyo, 900-1175.
Top right: Casa Riconda Plan. The kiva is a ceremonial space with four columns supporting the roof.
Bottom: "Great Kiva." New Mexico, Chaco/Anasazi, Chaco Canyon, plaza of Chetro Ketl, 900-1175.

Just as bees know how to make hives, and beavers know how to build dams, people seem to have an instinctual sense of how to build settlements. Looking at this wide variety of human settlement one notices certain recurring elements such as streets and the hierarchy of public squares and private interior places re-occur. This instinct is co-modified, however, by the environment and the culture's world view.

Our instinct for community building is modified by the resources and form of the place we are settling. The environment directs the use of materials—almost always wood, adobe or stone—and the physical layout of the village form. Villages in steep valleys run linearly along water; flat land villages tend to circle around a central well; seacoast villages semicircle around a natural harbor.

Finally, in addition to the force of instinct and the influence of the environment, the third force that consistently shapes settlements is the culture's understanding of the relationship between man and nature. In culture after culture of natural peoples, there is a continuity between their understanding of nature and their own consciousness. In the Anasazi village, the village form is based on a map of the universe. There is total continuity of meaning between world view, mythology, and the form of the village. In such a place, one always knows where one is. A door faces east because that is not only where the sun rises, but where mythic journeys begin. When one sets out for the day, one sets out in one's own footsteps and in the footsteps of all previous mythological forbears.

Vincent Scully has eloquently described how in settlements as diverse as Pueblo villages, Mesoamerican and Mesopotamian cities, and ancient Crete the physical form of the city reflects its people's understanding of their relationship to their environment. These communities are often reflections of the nearby sacred mountains. Scully claims that the Greeks in the late seventh century B.C. "confronted the divinity of the earth...with the human determination to be special in the world, different from the rest of creation."[10] Thus Athens, the human city, triumphed over the earth rather than being at harmony with the earth. Later, "Rome turned inward and elected, at least, to create an ideal universe within, closed off from the natural world."[11] Contemporary Western civilization thus inherited from Greece and Rome a culture of separation from, rather than integration with, the world. When Rome declined, it did so in an astonishing display of violence and materialism. By the year 300, there were enough seats in the Roman Colosseums and gathering places for *50%* of the population to watch gladiators and other spectacles of death, and 200 public holidays on which to do so. As the great civic culture of Rome declined, it was replaced by a self-indulgent one. Every man for the city was replaced by every man for himself.[12]

In The Structure of Scientific Revolutions, Thomas Kuhn suggested that culture evolves through deep changes of world view. These changes come from new ways of understanding the functioning of the universe, and man's relation to it.

Ages have ruling scientific or worldview paradigms, which shape culture. We are just emerging from a Cartesian/Newtonian paradigm, which produced a mechanistic, materialistic understanding of how the world works. When mixed with Locke and Darwin, the result was the survival of the fittest, property rights and American planning.

The emerging paradigms of the 20th century are relativity, chaos theory and ecology. We are now experiencing the cultural disturbances of the paradigm transformation. Its effect on planning will be to move from a paradigm of the individual against the system to one of consensus building.[8]

In the Taos pueblo, as in all pueblos, the man-made pyramid of North House is symmetrical in shape, but still clearly echoes the masses of Taos Mountain, and its fabricated abstraction of natural forms is still believed to help the mountain give up its water to the never failing stream that flows down through the center of the place. Seen from the side, North House also rises straight up to a typical pueblo sky altar, echoing and abstracting the shapes of the clouds, so that the dances that take place before it, their drum and foot beats built into the setback forms, are dancing the mountain, dancing the cloud...perhaps affecting the course of nature itself, and drawing all together into a pressure cooker of power, which the human city has always felt itself to be.[9]
-Vincent Scully

There is currently emerging a relationship between the infrastructure of our settlements and the corresponding culture, and the actual computer hardware and software. As we weave more networks across the earth, we actually may be weaving a new, human built proto-organism, of which those of us connected by the internet are merely cells. We think we have free will, and yet none of us is actually designing this larger network. Its form seems to be evolving in the same pattern of development as did the neurological systems of the chain of species.

The spacing of the ribbed patterns on the bottom of a stream are caused by the motion of the water over the sand. Does the flowing water or the inert sand have intention? The clusters of cars on a highway, and the spaces between them, exactly duplicate the proportions between the ribs of sand, Each driver thinks he has intention to go faster or slower, yet the overall pattern of the cars is the same as an "unintentional" pattern.

We are now weaving a network of information carriers (telephone, computer networks, cable, etc.). Our system started out as a crude telegraph system, but it is racing towards ever increasing complexity. The pattern of growth is duplicating the evolution of neurological systems from the most primitive to the human brain and nervous system.

As this system evolves, it will have an enormous impact on our relationship to the earth. Perhaps we will consume less material as we spend more money to consume information and data-based entertainment.

Will we travel less because we work and shop by computer? Will we become disenfranchised, or liberated to be more at home in our communities? What forces will shape our settlements? Perhaps our current suburban settlement pattern is a reflection of the telephone as much as the automobile. With the automobile we still need streets; with the telephone, we transcend them. And thus, as our social intercourse moves into the interior of the house, streets merely become ways of access, and we lose the street as the communications network of community. [16]

If the physical form of a city is its hardware and the culture of a city is its software, there is a co-evolving relationship between the hardware and the software of cities. The hardware is the physical, constructed environment: the infrastructure of roads, utilities, transportation systems and public places. Urban software is the social culture that defines the way people live in the city's environment. [13]

We can also see this relationship between physical form and culture in the economic growth in cities. As cultures urbanize, individuals tend to develop specialized skills. Specialization leads to a burgeoning of crafts and arts, the growth of workshops, and the development of specialized markets. This specialization leads to economic and social hierarchies. The urbanistic manifestation is the advent of the shop, the storehouse, the merchant class, and the merchant home. As wealth is gained and stored (cities tend to be storehouses of wealth) the economic value of the product of skilled workers and clever traders grows. This economic diversification is reflected in diversification of home size and type. However, as the economic system grows, it replaces the religious map of the universe with an economic paradigm, which fosters a materialistic culture less capable of providing the sense of connection and meaning which the more universal model previously satisfied. Furthermore, the economic model fosters a more uniform urban plan which is applied with less sensitivity to the local ecology or customs.

The green revolution has taught us the genetic poverty of monocultures. As the suburbs have grown, our downtowns have become a monoculture, as witnessed by the declining diversity of building types. Contemporary regions whose hardware lacks an integration of office and housing have downtowns that empty at five PM: such places lack a civic culture. Cities that mix downtown jobs and a range of residential options tend to have thriving theaters, concert halls, bars and galleries, and a greater sense of civitas.

Anton Neesan studied citizen reaction to contemporary development. He showed slides of a broad range of settlement patterns to residents in hundreds of communities and discovered a great concurrence as to the kind of places viewers wanted to live in. When given an opportunity to "vote" on which slides like best, most Americans chose those showing places like the winding streets of Nantucket, the squares of early Spanish-American settlements, and New England villages. Few liked the tree-barren, six-lane wide arterials edged by Wal-Marts and neon-lit fast food joints. [14] It is odd that contemporary American zoning codes make it impossible to build the landscape that most citizens actually want, and legislate the development of that they least like. No wonder no one wants new developments. We have given up the quality of village-scale street widths in exchange for arterials designed to accommodate nuclear evacuations; in the process, we have nuked our communities.

Most suburban and rural planning winds up in the hands of volunteer boards who have ceded the quality of their communities to professional planners. These planners, in turn, apply highway standards to the design of roads, which constitute a predominant share of the public realm. In commercial districts these roads are then lined with shopping centers which have been shaped by the rigid auto-oriented design standards of national retail chains. Lenders will gladly finance a single-story building leased to a national credit tenant, but are loath to finance mixed-use projects with smaller local tenants: what gets financed is what gets built.[15] Thus, the developments in the suburbs of Birmingham, Alabama and Belleview, Washington look exactly the same. In each case the public realm is relegated to a parking lot.

Houses make a town, but citizens a city.[18]
-Rousseau

As designers and developers, we have a responsibility to examine what kind of culture we are forming when we design and build. What culture is provided by the current highway-oriented system of metropolitan form? Amory Lovins says, "The best way to achieve access is to already be there."[17] When people live a more pedestrian life, they connect more, and a more vibrant, interactive culture arises. As we search for alternate forms of viable cities and suburbs, what new cultures are we creating? The "neo-traditionalists" are very fond of porches as a way of bringing the family to face the civic realm, but this is not enough. Following the model of healthy organic systems, communities need to be diverse, flexible, and integrated into their environment. Thus our neighborhoods should integrate a variety of ages, family types, and income groups. We need to mix places of living, working, learning, and reflecting. Our communities must also remind us of the social contract, or they will dissipate.

Televisions, automobiles, and the rest of the hardware comprising our material culture have an unmistakable impact on the way we interact or fail to interact with each other. There is a significant difference between running into someone while strolling down a street, and running into someone while driving a car. As urbanists we are interested in building communities; we have used the debate between the pedestrian and the auto as a shorthand for interaction versus isolation. That is also why we like a mix of uses. But we must ask ourselves: what more can we do to make communities places of connection?

We need to make explicitly state those values we wish to inculcate. The old New England town had a square (commons) in its center, and around it were four buildings: the library, the court house, the town hall and the church. The green represented nature as the common good, and it was defined by buildings embodying knowledge (library), justice (courthouse), governance (town hall) and spirit (church). In the town center one interacts with and absorbs knowledge and values from these buildings. Such a center

Plato says that in opposition to the ideal state, "if you also wish to see a State at fever heat, I have no objection. For I suspect that many will not be satisfied with the simpler way of life. They will be for adding sofas and tables and other furniture: also dainties and perfumes and incense and courtesans and cakes." [19]

While "Sustainability" has become a catchword in development and in environmental circles, it must be acknowledged that contemporary civilization and its patterns of land use and resource consumption are simply unsustainable. Add in world population growth, and it becomes hard to imagine long term sustainability. At best we can be more environmentally responsible about our work. [20]

continually re-imbues the local culture with its values. If we can determine how to bring these five values—knowledge, justice, governance, spirit and common good—back into what we build, we will go a long way toward making better places.

Today our centers are always dominated by retail, reflecting the materialism that is at our cultural center. For Americans, shopping is a ritual which affirms a positive cultural experience. Who can go to a museum and resist the urge to shop on the way out? Major arenas are leased to rock concert promoters for a percentage of the T-shirt sales rather than ticket sales, because the T-shirts often provide more income. As architects, planners and developers, we must ask ourselves if we are building retail which stimulates commerce and craft between people, or which isolates them. Trade can be a healthy human endeavor. In it one finds the commerce of ideas and interactions that weave a community together. People yearn for this stimulation. It is said that Biblical prophesy could only exist in communities where there were marketplaces in which to make proclamations to crowds. Studies indicate that people in Seattle would much rather shop in the Pike Place Public Market than in a supermarket. Shopping at Pike Place may mean paying higher prices, but people are eleven times as likely to talk to a stranger in Pike Place Market as they are in a supermarket checkout line. But retail can also be destructive: a Wal-Mart on the edge of a town destroys small business; it transforms local entrepreneurs into employees. It replaces locally made products with national ones. It replaces the pharmacist who knows your doctor and your family with one who probably does not.

We need to create an economic development paradigm that focuses on livelihoods rather than jobs. A livelihood is meaningful work that supports needs, but also supports a sustainable, holistic world view. Indigenous people did not merely have jobs—their livelihood was integrated into a much more imaginative sense of how to live pleasurably without destroying the world they lived in.

The root cause of all environmental impacts is consumption of energy, materials, and land. As developers, planners, and architects we are in the business of promoting consumption: by consuming land, by consuming building materials, and by making places where people consume. Solar-heated greenhouses built on rich agricultural soils, displacing productive farms, are not the paradigms of sustainability they have been lauded as. We need to capture the imbedded materials and energy in our existing communities. It is often inappropriate to destroy open lands because we cannot be bothered to reconstitute aging cities and suburbs. If we really believe in sustainability, then we have an obligation to ask ourselves if what we build is really necessary. Not every piece of land need be developed. Not every center needs retail, and not every store sells

Pike Place Market.

Above: Bergen Street Garden.
Below: Manhattan Graveyard.

goods that further our culture. As Plato posits in *The Republic*, the ideal world is one of enlightenment and satisfaction in which we live comfortably but do not exceed our means. War comes from the yearning for a more luxurious state.[21] Is it intrinsic to the nature of Western culture to seek luxury rather than the common good?

We need to re-connect our communities with nature, and we need to map natural systems in the design of our places. Too often, environmental planning simply means leaving steep slopes and creeks as undeveloped residual spaces, considered too difficult to develop. In almost every case, rather than seeing this space as an opportunity to bring sacredness into the community, or even just as a good place for kids to play, these natural spaces have been treated as drainage ditches.

Most planners merely talk about making good transit and traffic connections. Wildlife and natural lands also need good connections if their biological systems are to be viable. One interesting indicator of the health of our places is the frequency of return of migratory species. Migratory species weave connections between several environments, often the place of birth and the place they live in maturity, or between their winter and summer feeding grounds. Migratory species have paths that connect their journey. Thus we often find birds using the marshes of our West Coast cities as resting places on their journey from Canada to Mexico. As we impact the ecology of our planet through development, it is manifested as impediments to these migratory routes. On the other hand, where we make place for these species in our communities, they are enriched. It is no coincidence that migratory species often figure in the place-defining mythologies of ritual peoples.[22]

How can we bring ritual and sacred open space into our cities and villages? While ritual and sacredness have not played significant roles in the foundation of our contemporary American ethos, we can find seeds of places of ritual to build upon. Urban graveyards are places that are fenced, creating a sense of safety and protection against violence—but they are also green, natural spaces. Perhaps most importantly, they are sacred places for their communities, bringing people back again and again to think about the past and about continuity. They bind families to place. Is it natural, in the same way it is natural for salmon to be born and die in the same place, for humans to return to their places of birth? Is this why in so many of the pre-literate epics, the hero's journey takes him home again?

Community gardens reconnect people with land, with life, and with cycles of growth. In community gardens, people may again work the earth or simply enjoy it. Older generations can transmit to younger ones the culture of working with one's hands, and of raising things from the earth. Perhaps, most importantly, people can meet in a safe, neutral public space.[23]

In the abandoned, burned out blocks of Home Street in the South Bronx, one finds small community gardens, laid out in crosses, and decorated with mixtures of Catholic and Caribbean ritualistic symbols. It is interesting that as local residents took control of abandoned property and converted it into public places, the first constructions were clearly formed places of renewal (gardens) and places of return (graveyards).

We know something is missing in our contemporary metropolises. Many of our cities no longer reflect their local environment. It has been a long time since our cities have been made of local materials. Since our plans are based on economics— our new map of the universe—our instincts are overruled by technocratic zoning and the preferences of our financial credit system. The result is an anomie which, depending on one's background, is expressed through materialism or violence. The path back to a co-evolving form of community is to design organically, acknowledging our archetypal settlement pattern and the environment in which we build, and to rethink our values, mapping them deeply in our places.

NOTES

1,2 The application of thermodynamics and the rules of organic growth to planning and development is not taken from any source directly, but rather is a synthesis of my thoughts in these two areas since 1970. For further information, I suggest the following sources: Nicholas Georgescu-Roegen, *The Entropy Law and the Economic Process* (Cambridge: Harvard University Press, 1971); Harold F. Blum, *Time's Arrow and Evolution*, third edition (Princeton: Princeton University Press, 1968); Stephen Jay Gould, *Time's Arrow, Time's Cycle* (Cambridge: Harvard University Press, 1987); Teilhard De Chardin, *The Phenomenon of Man* (New York: Harper and Row, 1959).

3 Based on gross leasable retail space in the United States in 1964 and 1992 respectively, divided by United States populations in those years. Gross leasable area data provided by the International Council of Shopping Centers, and based on materials published and/or researched by Shopping Center World magazine, Monitor magazine and the National Research Bureau. For further information on methodology, etc., contact the NRB located in Chicago. Population data from U.S. Bureau of the Census, Current Population Reports, 25-311, 25-1045, and 25-1097. Between 1978 and 1987, the population of the United States increased by 9.6% while gross retail space increased by 35.7%, nearly four times as fast. International Council of Shopping Centers and U. S. Census Bureau.

4 Nicholas Davidson, "Life Without Father—America's Greatest Social Catastrophe." *Policy Review*, no. 51, winter 1990, 40-44.

5 "Cease Fire in the War Against Children," Children's Defense Fund, 25 E Street, NW, Washington, DC 20001, 1992.

6 Malidoma Some, "Rites of Passage," *Utne Reader*, July/August 1994, 67-68.

7 Mircea Eliade, *The Sacred and the Profane.*

8 Thomas Kuhn, *The Structure of Scientific Revolutions* (Chicago: University of Chicago Press, 1970).

9-11 Vincent Scully, "Mankind and Earth in America and Europe," in *The Ancient Americas: Art from Sacred Landscapes.* (Chicago: Art Institute of Chicago, 1992).

12 See generally: Edward Gibbon, *The Decline and Fall of the Roman Empire* (New York: Viking Penguin Inc., 1987); Edward Mumford, *The City in History* (New York: Harcourt Brace Jovanovich, 1989).

13,16 The author was the first person to develop live/work environments that integrated hardware, software and access to information as standard utilities. The American Thread Building in Tribeca, New York, was built with a computer terminal and on-line services in every residential unit, anticipating how work would be done from home years before the invention of the Macintosh and the P.C. The metaphor of hardware and software as built and cultural environments which were co-determined has been a long-time theme of the author's career and writings; the first place it was publicly expressed was at the first meeting of the Congress for the New Urbanism in 1993.

14 Visual preference studies conducted by Anton Nelessen, an architect and planner who works in Princeton, N. J., show that in terms of people's preferences for how communities should be laid out, "A set of design principles is constant, in spite of regional differences." Nelessen says that in general, participants "hate commercial strips, arterial roads, and are anti-sprawl." See *Architectural Record*, May 1994, 29.

15 For more information on this effect see Constance El Beaumont, *How Superstore Sprawl Can Harm Communities* (Washington, D.C.: National Trust for Historic Preservation, 1994).

17 In a speech given at a conference of the Social Venture Network, March 1994.

18 Jean Jacques Rousseau, *The Social Contract*, Trans. G. D. H. Cole (New York: E. P. Dutton & Company, Inc., 1950), Book 1, note 1, 15.

19 Plato, *The Republic*, Trans. B. Jowett, M.A. (New York: Vintage Books, 1983), Book II, no. 373, 65.

20 See my forthcoming essay in Progressive Architecure, to be published in the Spring of 1995.

21 Plato, Book VIII.

22 For more information contact Christina Desser at The Migratory Species Project, 414.567.6328.

23 For more information on urban gardens contact the Trust for Public Land at 802.649.3611.

FIGURE CREDITS

Frontis Courtesy of Author's collection.

1 *Conquest: Montezuma, Cortes, and the Fall of Old Mexico* by Hugh Thomas (New York: Simon and Schuster, 1993).

2 Courtesy Phoenix Art Museum.

3 Richard Townsend, ed., The Ancient Americas : Art from Sacred Landscapes (Chicago : The Art Institute of Chicago, 1992), Photo by Richard Townsend.

4 By permission of The British Library, G 7032 (2,3).

5 Courtesy Phoenix Art Museum.

3,4 Photographs by Richard Farmer.

5 Photo by Ken Sherman.

6 Photo by A. Inzer.

NOVUS ORDO SECLORUM:
THE COUNTY COURTHOUSE AS OBJECT AND SYMBOL

MATTHEW J. BELL

Matthew J. Bell is Assistant Professor of Architecture at the University of Maryland at College Park.

We have seen that in the United States, there was no administrative centralization. There is scarcely a trace of a hierarchy. There decentralization has been carried to a degree that no European nation would tolerate, I think, without profound discomfort...

Alexis de Tocqueville, *Democracy in America*.[1]

Travelling across 20th century America, through the vast scene of physical disorder the past century or so has fostered, one can still find traces of an eighteenth century landscape that is, by comparison, highly ordered in form and meaning. Leaving the disorienting din of the suburbs one first encounters a gridded rural landscape, and then the gridded small town, often centered by a square or park lined by stores, a post office, a town hall, and other social and civic institutions. Following almost forgotten eighteenth century roads one is likely to discover county courthouses and courthouse squares along the way. Remnants of an earlier time, they stand as records of the values and ideas that shaped them; forms that embody and convey an ideal notion of American society.

This ideal derives from inherited values of the Old World as well as values evolved from a new American context. While European ideals have had major influences on American institutions, their significance lies primarily in the unique intellectual and physical context to which they have been applied. The structure of traditional archetypal political forms, such as the Constitution, have been adapted from older models to new circumstances and purposes. Even foundation mythologies, such as those relating to the life of the "father" of the country, George Washington, provide instruction for the citizen and foster a national faith and purpose, regardless of contemporary beliefs.

George Caleb Bingham, *The County Election*, 1852.

A similar transformation of social and political ideals can be seen in architectural and urban types. The image of a public building within an ideal town square, such as the centralized courthouse and square, has early roots in the civic projects of Italian cities in the fifteenth century. To begin with, there are obvious formal similarities between an ideal Renaissance church and square and almost any midwestern central courthouse square (figs. 1, 2).[2] In each situation a centralized temple is placed in the center of a public square, the limits of which are clearly demarcated by building fabric, and located within a ordered field of buildings and streets.

The American courthouse and square differ, however, from their fifteenth century counterparts in several obvious ways. First, the center is occupied by the headquarters of local and regional government; it is a secular rather than a religious building. Second, the space which surrounds the courthouse is not the dense, urban piazza of European origins, but rather a quotation of the pastoral landscape of the American countryside.

Third, the urban space of the Renaissance church or temple was most often approached via a system of axial streets, whereas the archetypal American courthouse square occupies a block in the continuous grid of the town.

These seemingly simple formal differences can be seen as the physical manifestations of laws and ideas unique to the New World, and provide insight into the relationship of local government to the quasi-religious myths of the new nation. As authors Paige Smith and Conrad Cherry have described, the secularization of religious myth and its transformation into national values and beliefs has spurred an evolution of civic architecture in the United States, from domestic models of the early colonial period to types traditionally associated with centuries of western religious architecture. What are the origins of this tradition? Has the transformation succeeded in producing a truly American urban and architectural type? Does this account satisfy the traditional American resistance to centralized authority on the one hand while upholding the principles of democratic government?

1. Santa Maria della Consolazione, Todi, Italy, 1508.

2. Anderson County Courthouse, Palestine, Texas.

ORIGINS

Seventeenth century colonial governors of the Virginia colony passed several acts encouraging the development of cities and towns. Such settlements were thought to be more economically viable, easier to defend and more politically stable than small villages and agricultural estates. In 1634 the colonial legislature created nine shires or counties and fixed them as the unit of local government. This type of government structure dates back to a system of county offices established after the Norman conquest of England in 1066.[3]

Initially, Virginia's county governments held court and legislative sessions in private homes and local taverns. However, early colonial leaders such as Francis Nicholson, the designer of Williamsburg and Annapolis, strongly advocated the construction of courthouses.[4]

Throughout the seventeenth century courthouses were built in each county and were ideally placed equidistant from the surrounding plantations.[5] In many instances these locations were a great distance from any town, and even today many courthouses remain quite rural. One of the earliest appearances of a courthouse sited within a town is in Williamsburg. Here, the courthouse occupied a prominent location on the main thoroughfare. Inherent in Williamsburg's town plan is the tension between the presence of colonial power, the Governor's Palace, and local authority represented by the courthouse.[6]

In the eighteenth century, as the Virginia colony began to establish small towns, courthouses tended to be given central locations in the town plan. Often developed as a garden or a walled keep, the open space of the courthouse square provided relief from the urban grid which characterized the planning of Virginia towns of this period. In Leesburg, Virginia, founded in 1758, the courthouse was located on the corner of the central intersection of the town plan (fig. 3).

In New England the courthouse square or green evolved out of the tradition of the Congregational or Puritan meeting house.

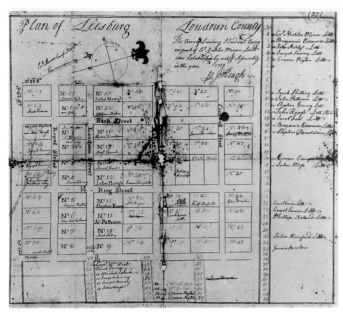

3. Plan of Leesburg, Loudoun County, Virginia, 1759.

The meeting house served as the place where the religious life of the community was consecrated and also where all civic decisions were made by the town elders. This interdependence of religious and secular responsibilities descended directly from the medieval English village tradition.[7] The townspeople would assemble in the meeting house on Sundays for worship, and meet again in the same location during the week to decide civil matters. As multiple religious groups were established in the town, the meeting house lost its sole association with one religious group and was used to decide all civil matters. Public activities such as criminal punishment, commercial trade, and military exercises also occurred on the town green adjacent to the meetinghouse (fig. 4).

The location and character of the meeting house in the New England town draws its form from the market hall of medieval England.[8] Frequently the English market building contained a hall or large room on the second level used for civil proceedings and religious lectures. Unlike churches, which were placed to the side of a street or plaza, the medieval English market hall was

4. **Salem Common on Training Day.**

usually found in the center of a street or public space.[9] Similarly, the New England meeting house either faced the center of the town green, as at Ipswich, Massachusetts (fig. 6), or was placed in the space of the green itself, as at Salem (fig. 7).[10] Symbolically, the town green occupied a higher part of the local landscape while commercial buildings were located along low lying routes easily accessible to surrounding agricultural holdings or to sources of water. The high visibility of the meeting house, its tower or spire rising above the collection of commercial and domestic buildings, provided a physical image of the social and religious order of the community.

As these towns grew, churches of other denominations occupied sites in or at the edge of the town green. It was not uncommon to find several churches and meeting houses sitting side-by-side (fig. 5). Unlike the systematic development of the Virginia county, the New England meeting house could be found in almost every incorporated community, regardless of size or distance to the next one.

Another early influence in the development of the court-house town can be traced to fifteenth century theories of the ideal city, transported from Italy through England to the New World in the seventeenth century.[11] The designs for Savannah, Philadelphia, and New Haven have all been recognized as derivatives of Vitruvian planning. The original New Haven plan of 1638 adheres to many Vitruvian town planning principles such as the relationship to landscape features seen in the orientation of streets to prevailing winds.[12] A central open space was designated for public buildings; during the eighteenth century this space contained a market and the meeting house (fig. 8). The plan of Savannah provided for institutional buildings to face public spaces, although the location of the courthouse was not originally assigned.

The Philadelphia plan of 1682 served as a model for many county seats established in eighteenth-century Pennsylvania (fig. 9). The bi-laterally symmetrical plan included a central square intended for a public building or meeting house, with additional public squares in each quadrant of the plan. The central square was approached on all four sides by a wide street; the Market and

5.. Leicester, Massachusetts in the nineteenth century.

6.. North Common or Green, Ipswich, Massachusetts.

Broad Streets of today, which intersected the square on axis. John Reps cites the 1622 plan of Londonderry, Northern Ireland as one probable source for the Philadelphia plan. Similar to the centralized Philadelphia plan, the center of the main public space in the Londonderry plan was at one time occupied by a market, a prison and a town hall all under one roof.[13] Variations of this urban plan type proliferated throughout eastern and central Pennsylvania. Two examples are Wilkes-Barre, founded in 1772, and Bedford (1766), which were both organized around similar central squares. Lancaster, Pennsylvania was founded by a colony of settlers from Philadelphia under the leadership of William Penn's son Thomas Penn; its public square was taken directly from the Philadelphia model (fig. 10). The courthouse square was placed on a small hill overlooking the surrounding territory, at the exact intersection of the town's principal cross streets.

Most of the eighteenth-century towns designed according to the Philadelphia model were colonies of the original Pennsylvania colony and were intended to expand the Quaker territory westward. Colonial building types and town planning methods

7. A Street in Salem, Massachussetts in 1765.

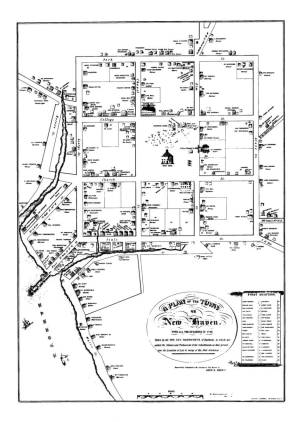

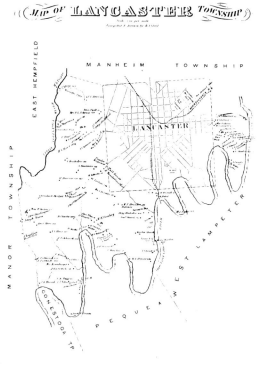

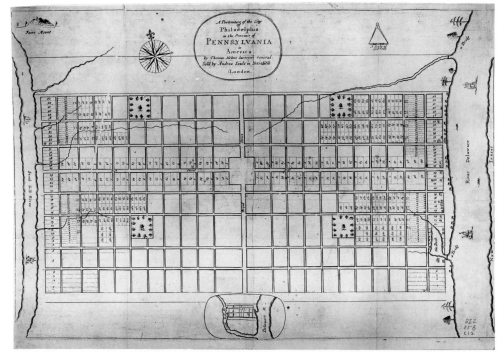

8. New Haven, Connecticut in 1824.

9. Plan of Lancaster, Pa., 1875.

10. William Penn's Plan for Philadelphia, Pennsylvania, 1682.

were disseminated via settlement routes to the territories west of the Allegheny Mountains.[14] The Philadelphia/Lancaster plan was transported west and south to other parts of the country. According to Edward T. Price, many of the towns bearing the names Lancaster and Philadelphia in Ohio, Kentucky and South Carolina share attributes of the Pennsylvania model.[15]

East coast meeting house and town square types were also dispersed westward by the movement of settlers from Massachusetts and Connecticut to Ohio and lands further west. This migration gave many small towns in Ohio, particularly the lands of the former Western Reserve, such as Tallmadge, Ohio, a decidedly New England appearance (fig. 11).[16] Consequently, many courthouse squares built in counties of the Western Reserve of Ohio and areas further west are similar in form to Colonial New England meeting houses, early courthouses and churches.

URBAN DEVELOPMENTS AFTER 1785

The Land Ordinance of 1785 organized the land west of the original thirteen colonies into townships of thirty-six square miles and then grouped them together to form a county (fig. 12). Unlike New England towns, which had a medieval and picturesque layout, towns and counties founded after the survey of 1785 were almost exclusively organized on a grid.

The six-mile-square agricultural township became the fundamental meter in these new territories. Earlier proposed units ranged from ten square miles, suggested in the first draft of the committee of the Continental Congress chaired by Thomas Jefferson in 1784, to the five square miles employed in the Western Reserve lands of Ohio. Although use of the six-by-six square mile township as the ideal township organization dates back to the early colonies, such an organization provided no place

11. View of the Central Green in Tallmadge, Ohio, 1874.

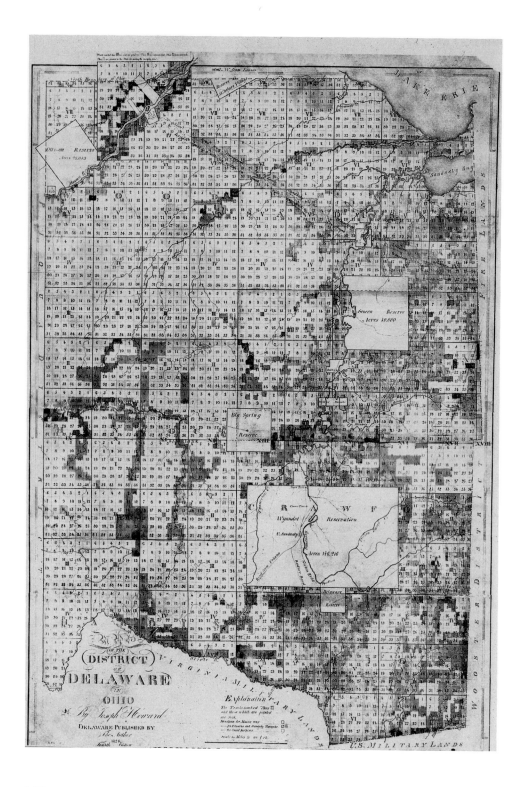

12. District of Delaware, Ohio, 1824.

for a center within the township proper. The county structure adheres to an even less systematic order, sometimes composed of three-square-mile townships, and other times as large as four- or five-square-mile townships.

The courthouse town was typically placed in the center of the county, equidistant from neighboring county seats. The courthouse, located at the center of a public square, became an immediate symbol of the town's participation in the government of the developing nation. Locating the county seat in a new town was a source of great competition between new towns, because having the county courthouse virtually guaranteed some degree of economic prosperity.

Throughout the expansion of the post-colonial period, land speculation ran rampant as the country became involved in a self-conscious effort to establish and enlarge itself. Speculators often designated one or several squares for public use in the town plan hoping that the county seat would be attracted there. This settlement pattern was commonly found in Ohio (statehood in 1803), Indiana (1816), Texas (1845) and throughout the midwest, particularly in states admitted to the union in the first half of the nineteenth century. A good example is the town of Fort Worth, the county seat of Tarrant County, Texas, which locates the courthouse in the center of a pair of square blocks (fig. 13). This adjustment to the pattern of blocks and open space in the town aligns the principal street axially with the courthouse. Denton, Texas follows a similar arrangement where the grid of the town adjusts to allow the two major streets of the town to enter the space on axis with all four sides of the courthouse building.

County courthouses built after the first period of expansion in this country descended from earlier colonial models but with several important differences. The buildings were centralized or square in configuration, and most courthouses were placed at the center of the town plan. Finally, as an economic unit of a town and township, the building became the functional and emblematic center of the entire county, not simply of the small town and its immediate agricultural holdings.

BUILDING TYPES

Public buildings in the early New England colonies can be traced to the civic and domestic architecture of the medieval English village.[17] The meeting house was either square or rectangular in plan with a second floor gallery reached by a tower at the end of the building or by an interior stair. In the rectangular building type, the long side typically faced the town green with the entrance at the center of the facade. The Old-Ship Meeting-House in Hingham, Massachusetts of 1681 has a four-square plan and closely resembles many of the adjacent houses (fig. 14). Meeting houses possesed important architectural features, such as a cupola or stair tower which distinguished it as a public building. Most meeting houses of the seventeenth and eighteenth centuries lacked decorative elements, which were generally considered unessential for religious structures. Many of the first public buildings constructed in the midwest, such as the first state house in Chillicothe, Ohio, closely resembled the early meeting houses of New England.

The first models for the Virginia courthouses, like those of the New England colonies, were derived from domestic architecture.[18] An exterior loggia or piazza was typically used to distinguish the civic house of the early government from the dwelling house.[19] Many of these structures were built with a walled enclosure, as at Gloucester, the county seat of Gloucester County, Va. These enclosures may be related to the walled compound of the plantation, as at Stratford Hall. The public space of the courthouse was organized as a small compound containing several smaller buildings which housed many different county offices. This system of organization continued well into the nineteenth century.

As the United States evolved from a country of separate religious and secular communities to a unified nation, government buildings began more literally to adapt and employ the forms of ecclesiastical architecture. The longitudinal house-like form of earlier meeting houses evolved in the eighteenth century

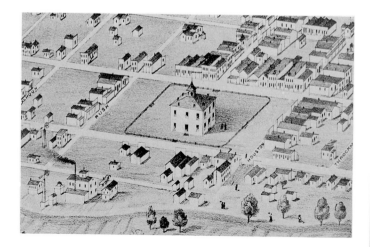

15. Old White Meeting house, Strafford, Vermont, 1799.
16. Missouri Counties and county seats after 1876.

into the neoclassical temple form. The short end of the building turned toward the public space and incorporated the tower into the pediment of the facade (fig. 15). Later versions of the New England meeting house and the mid-western courthouse are often indistinguishable from the town's churches.

From the early to the mid-nineteenth century, the courthouse had typologically evolved from the Greek Revival temple to the centralized and often domed courthouses of the later century. However, from the middle to the end of the nineteenth century, courthouses were often built in a Romanesque or Classical centralized form, not unlike the ideal centralized church of the fifteenth century. This centralized form seems to transcend stylistic issues. Courthouses with similar centralized configurations can be found in a variety of architectural styles.

The 1785 ordinance theoretically provided an ideal arrangement of equal and regularly sized agricultural townships. After these areas were surveyed and settled, boundaries were adjusted to the irregularities of the landscape. County seats were then established at the general center of the county (fig. 16).[20] In terms of political structure, each of the states admitted to the union under the earlier Ordinance of 1784 initially had to adopt the constitution of one of the original thirteen colonies prior to becoming a state. This law in effect transferred the pattern of political structure which had evolved in the east to the midwest and beyond.[21]

Thus these new counties organized their townships in much the same way as the original colonies. Urbanistically, the new courthouse was the center of both the county and of the surrounding agricultural townships (fig. 17). This settlement pattern produced highly centralized formal relationships ranging in scale from the organization of the agricultural landscape to the form and location of the county seat itself.

Changes in architectural and urban paradigms encouraged centralized building types. The United States Capitol building, and later the buildings of the World's Colombian Exposition, became important paradigms for many courthouses built up until

17. Courthouse and Grid System, Plainview, Texas.

the first World War. In L'Enfant's plan of 1790, the Capitol dominated the skyline and could be approached with the same grandeur from any direction. State capital buildings were often modeled on the U. S. Capitol with a central dome over a public lobby and with offices and meeting chambers in each wing. The dome, previously the most cogent symbol of traditional religious power since the Renaissance, was transformed to symbolize the ascendant power of the young republic. The county courthouse, in the form of a centralized building, could appear like the Capitol in miniature, equally central to all citizens in its jurisdiction (fig. 20).

A new variation of the courthouse type was originated in the nineteenth century by Texas architect James Riely Gordon. The relationship between the building and the street system was

18. View of Luzerne County Courthouse.
19. View of Dome, Luzerne County Courthouse, Wilkes-Barre, Pa.

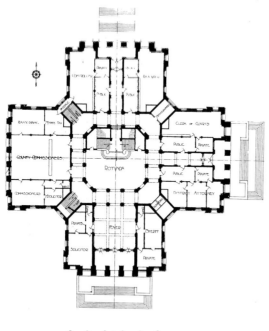

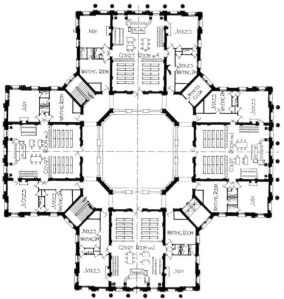

20. Ground Floor Plan, Luzerne County Courthouse, Wilkes-Barre, Pa.
21. View of Dome, Luzerne County Courthouse, Wilkes-Barre, Pa.

transformed by rotating the building with respect to the street grid. For example, the Ellis County Courthouse in Waxahachie, Texas places an entry at each of the four corners of the building, facing the four intersections surrounding the square (fig. 23). This modified orientation to the street presented an elongated facade—the two sides of the centralized building—to the actual entry of the square (fig. 22). These courthouses seem to acknowledge the primacy of the undifferentiated grid, as the building itself becomes an ideal object, capable of being entered from all sides and residing at the center of a continuous system of streets and blocks. The front of the building becomes the corner, seen on the oblique, and in these examples entered from that side as well.

The development of the centralized building in the county seat allowed for the building to represent its jurisdiction equally. Roads and streets emanated orthogonally from the courthouse in all directions. The square could be approached from almost any direction or place in the county with equal importance. The frontality of earlier longitudinal temple types, which by their formal characteristics inherently favored a specific direction, were inappropriate for these new counties. The orientation of the building, its dome or clock tower visible to all citizens, provided the practical amenities of a centralized organization, and the myth of unbiased connection to all parts of the county.

LANDSCAPE MYTHS AND IDEALS

In *Wilderness and the American Mind*, Roderick Nash explores beliefs about the wilderness held by the earliest colonists of the seventeenth and early eighteenth centuries, and their lasting imprint upon American thought.[22] According to Nash, these settlers ascribed to a Judeo-Christian cosmology that saw the wilderness as a fearful desolate place, symbolizing the banishment of the chosen people from the garden of paradise.[23] For

22. View of the Ellis County Courthouse, Waxahachie, Texas.

23. Plan of the Ellis County Courthouse, Waxahachie, Texas.

them, man's role was to conquer and order the wilderness, thereby extending the physical limits of the knowable world. This desire to subdue and order the natural world found its physical manifestation in the expanding American town and cultivated landscapes of the eighteenth and early nineteenth centuries. Like the many rationally ordered perspective scenes from the fifteenth century, the colonists employed the grid as the principle device to order the landscape. An early plan of Savannah indicates how the territory surrounding the town was to be organized (fig.24). The town was planned using a smaller grid with the landscape organized on a similar, yet larger, matrix. Garden and farm lots were extended from the common lands of the town proper to the surrounding countryside. Each "tything" was systematically squared and divided into twelve equal units and became the underlying grid for further development of the town.

This ordering of the great wilderness was for the early settlers a very real and pragmatic approach to reaffirming their existence and subduing nature. At another level, this new land of religious freedom was seen as analogous to the Holy Land of the New Jerusalem.[24] This myth infused the rhetoric of the earliest settlers with visions of the New World as the earthly incarnation of the Garden of Eden and the place of redemptive sacrifice and rebirth:

> Yes, God has designed a place for all his people. It is a spacious land. There will be room enough for all. There God's people will dwell like freeholders in a place of their own.[25]

As the growth of the American nation continued, these foundation myths and ideals evolved into a secular "religion" or "national faith." Combined with the Puritan belief in a divine mission from God, these foundation myths gave birth to what Conrad Cherry has referred to as a "civil religion."[26] Cherry cites the Declaration of Independence, the Constitution and the Bill of Rights as "covenants that bound together the people of the nation and secured to them God's blessing protection and call to historic

missions."[27] In Cherry's view, prominent individuals in the establishment or preservation of the freedom of the republic can be seen as analogous to Biblical figures. Washington, as the "deliverer of the American people out of bondage and the leader of the chosen people into the Promised Land of Independence," becomes both a Moses and a Joshua figure. Lincoln is seen as the Christ figure, tragically sacrificing himself for the preservation of the union.[28] Ceremonies such as Memorial Day, the Fourth of July, and Inauguration Day serve to reaffirm these myths annually.

The archetypal centralized courthouse is found in the center of a square surrounded by a garden landscape; a microcosm of the surrounding pastoral landscape of farms and countryside (figs. 25, 26). Often this space is the only significant public green space for many blocks or possibly even the entire county. While the piazza of the European city emphasized the urban aspect of its cosmology, its American counterpart acknowledged the agrarian, anti-urban foundations of the republic.[29] This image of the "New Jerusalem," embodied in the temple of justice and surrounded by an idealized image recalling the Garden of Eden, symbolizes the myth of God's covenant with his chosen people and the redemptive power of the pastoral landscape. If the church in Christian cosmology provided the locus for the sinner to receive redemptive justice and reclaim lost innocence, then the county courthouse provides the place where one's innocence may be maintained by a jury of his or her peers.

Dwelling in the pastoral or "middle" landscape, neither civilization nor wilderness, is consistent with communal values latent in American society.[30] Nature provides the origin of the town's wealth through its surrounding farms or ranches. In turn, this agrarian world sponsors the expansion of the town into a village of banks, schools and mercantile establishments. The town could not survive without its agrarian foundation. Thus, the courthouse and its square, the emblem of liberty and seat of local authority, are surrounded by the symbols of free enterprise and provide the continuing assurance of stability. As a microcosm of

24. Map of the County of Savannah, Georgia, 1735.

the national and state capital, each courthouse town appears as a little "utopia" in which the "rule of the law" is confronted with or supported by, the will of the people.[31]

Contrasting the finite boundaries of the ideal city, the American courthouse town has no clear physical limits and extends from the central square into the countryside. The town is united with its agrarian counterpart by a common grid. The center of the courthouse, signified by the dome, the tower or both, dominates the town skyline.

TRANSFORMATION OF MYTH AND BUILDING TYPE

Mircea Eliade in *The Myth of the Eternal Return* makes a distinction between traditional and historical man; traditional man renews his existence each year through the cyclical repetition of symbolic ceremonies and mythic stories which explain natural phenomena and offer "rebirth." In America, national holidays such as Inauguration Day, Memorial Day, or Independence Day, serve to reaffirm the tradition of the national faith.

25. Granite County Court House, Philipsburg, Montana, 1912.

26. Lee County Courthouse, Giddings, Texas, 1898.

These celebrations offer the symbolic abolition of time and promote the myth of the nation's eternal existence and rebirth. These rituals are performed within archetypal buildings and urban configurations, symbolizing the concentration of power, both real and imagined.

By contrast, historical man, according to Eliade, values historical events and sees time as a linear progression. He regards traditional conceptions of archetypes and symbolic myth as "... aberrant re-identifications of history."[32] He would therefore eschew the use of paradigms or historical types in favor of new forms of expression or novelties.

Most western societies from the Enlightenment to the twentieth century could probably be characterized as both traditional and historical. Twentieth century archetypal architectural and urban forms have been overwhelmed by the historically self-conscious avant-garde. At times, this has resulted in an anonymous representation of government, once an institution of unity which sought to provide and symbolize a common ground for people of diverse personal beliefs. Sadly, the architects of recent courthouses, and other governmental buildings for that matter, often reject any association with urban and architectural models so widely dispersed throughout the country in the last two centuries. Many small towns and county jurisdictions have seen their prominent public buildings rebuilt as county administration office buildings on the periphery of the town, surrounded by a sea of parking and lacking any association with the larger ideals and models which brought them into being. Traditional models are seen as inadequate or obsolete for a new society.[33]

If the architecture of the early United States embodied the national faith based on an ideal vision of a society—which was clearly in its initial stages—then how is the institutional building represented today? Public architecture serves now, instead, to conceal the presence of the institution, masking its size and downplaying any sense that government is indeed as powerful as it actually is.

The rise in individual prosperity in the United States has had an adverse effect upon the public realm. Historically, in societies where there was relatively little personal wealth, communal wealth aggrandized the institutions of local government and produced a highly charged symbolic architecture. Might the inverse also be true—that a society of increased personal wealth turns inward, unable or unwilling to invest in public architecture or in the public realm in general?

Much of the architecture of the "civil religion" that has been built in the last quarter century is notable for concealing its civic dimension. Institutions which formerly enjoyed a representative and symbolic architecture are now anonymous buildings immersed in the fabric of the city or even hidden in the landscape. What remains constant is the real power and status of the institution, with perhaps a corresponding adaptation of a functional building type, most often the office building as the building form.[34] Institutional building programs like the county courthouse, which previously employed cogent symbolic urban and architectural forms, seem to have been sublimated to a subversive role of maintaining the status quo and concealing authority. Public life, which depends partly upon the symbolic capacity of architecture to convey civic values, becomes the result of a more limited appropriation of building types—types which diminish the potential for architecture to play a symbolic and incisive role in a society both traditional and historical.

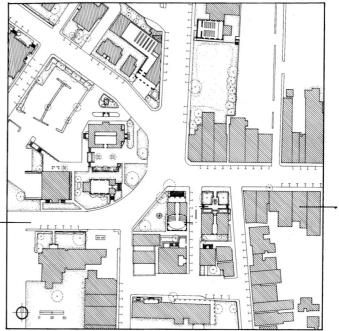

27. Site Plan of Fauquier County Courthouse Square, Warrenton, Va.

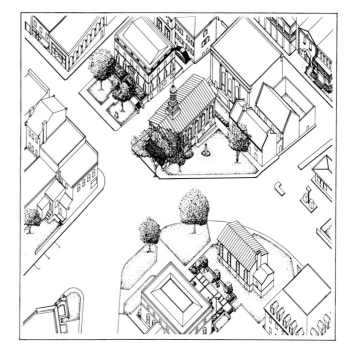

28. View of Fauquier County Courthouse Square, Warrenton, Va.

NOTES

1 Alexis de Tocqueville , *Democracy in America, 1848* (New York: Harper and Row, 1988), 89.

2 I owe this observation to Colin Rowe.

3 James D. Kornwolf, "Doing Good to Posterity, Francis Nicholson, First patron of Architecture, Landscape Design, and Town Planning in Virginia, Maryland and South Carolina, 1688-1725." *The Virginia Magazine of History and Biography* Vol. 101 No. 3, (July 1993): 339.

4 Kornwolf, "Doing Good to Posterity," 339.

5 Marcus Whiffen, "The Early County Courthouses of Virginia," *The Journal of the Society of Architectural Historians,* vol. 18, (March 1959): 2.

6 Kornwolf, "Doing Good to Posterity," 371.

7 Marian Card Donnelly, *The New England Meeting Houses of the Seventeenth Century* (Middletown, Conn.: Wesleyan University Press, 1968), 3.

8 Donnelly, *Meeting Houses*, 94.

9 Donnelly. *Meeting Houses.*

10 As early as 1637, there is evidence that meeting and courthouses were intended to be located in the center of a six square mile town. See Donnelly, 17.

11 For a complete discussion of the various courthouse square plan types see Edward T. Price, "The Central Courthouse Square in the American County Seat," *The Geographic Review,* Vol. LVIII 1968, reprinted in *Common Places: Readings in American Vernacular Architecture,* Ed. Dell Upton and John Michael Vlach, (London: The University of Georgia Press, 1986).

12 Anthony Garvan, *Architecture and Town Planning in Colonial Connecticut,* (New Haven: Yale University Press, 1951).

13 John Reps, *Town Planning in Frontier America* (Columbia: University of Missouri Press, 1980), 145.

14 Edward T. Price, "The Central Courthouse Square in the American County Seat," *The Geographic Review,* Vol. LVIII 1968: 40.

15 Price, "The Central Courthouse Square."

16 Reps, *Town Planning,* 246.

17 Donnelly, *Meeting Houses,*17.

18 Whiffen, "Early County Court- houses," 3.

19 Whiffen, "Early County Court- houses."

20 For a discussion of one state's founding of counties and the establish- ment of county seats, see Marian M. Ohman, *A History of Missouri's Counties, County Seats, and Courthouse Squares* (Columbia: University Extension division, University of Missouri Press, 1983).

21 Robert M. Taylor, ed., *The Northwest Ordinance 1787 A Bicentennial Handbook,* (Indianapolis: Indiana Historical Society, 1987) 18.

22 Roderick Nash, *Wilderness and the American Mind* (New Haven: Yale University Press, 1982), 8.

23 Nash, *Wilderness,* 24.

24 Nash, *Wilderness,* 25.

25 Ola Elizabeth Winslow, *Meeting- house Hill* (New York: MacMillan Company, 1952), 52.

26 Conrad Cherry, *God's New Israel: Religious Interpretations of American Destiny* (New Jersey: Prentice Hall, 1971), 26.

27 Cherry, *God's New Isreal.*

28 Cherry, *God's New Isreal,* 12.

29 Steven Hurtt, "The American Continental Grid: Form and Meaning," *Threshold,* vol. II, Autumn, 1983: 33.

30 Leo Marx, *The Machine in the Garden* (New York: Oxford University Press, 1964), 17-45.

31 Colin Rowe and John Hedjuk, "Lockhart, Texas," *Architectural Record* March 1957: 205.

32 Mircea Eliade, *The Myth of the Eternal Return* (Princeton: Princeton University Press, 1954) ,154.

33 Many of the first generation of modern architects, Le Corbusier for example, understood archetypal forms and how they might enrich and inform the building program. Corbu's work at Chandigarh and many of Aalto's public buildings incorporate archetypal architectural and urban forms.

34 Many of the county courthouses built in the post World War I decades depart significantly from the temple-type and typically employ the office building as a model for the building's form. Versions by Beaux-Arts trained architects were frequently modeled on the palazzo—for example the courthouses at Indianapolis and Milwaukee. Although this phenomena might be attributed to an increased complexity of building

FIGURE CREDITS

Frontis Courtesy of The Saint Louis Art Museum, Purchase.

1 Peter Murray, *Architecture of the Renaissance* (New York: Harry N. Abrams, Inc., Publishers).

2 Photo by Jeffrey Roberson.

3 Courtesy of the Geography and Map Division, Library of Congress, Washington, D.C.

4 Courtesy of Peabody & Essex Museum, Salem, MA.

5 Talbot Hamlin, *The American Spirit in Architecture* (New Haven: Yale University Press, 1926).

6 Talbot Hamlin, *The American Spirit in Architecture*.

7 Paul Zucher, *Town and Square: from the Agora to the Village Green* (New York: Columbia University Press, 1959).

8 Courtesy of New Haven Colony Historical Society.

9 Courtesy, Division of Rare and Manuscript Collections, Cornell University, Ithaca, New York.

10 *Atlas of Lancaster County Pennsylvania, 1875*.

11 Courtesy of Cornell University Library.

12 Joseph Howard, *The Mapping of Ohio* (Kent State University Press).

13 Willard B. Robinson, *The People's Architecture* (Texas State Historical Society).

14 Wayne Andrews, *Architecture in New England* (Brattleboro, Vermont: The Stephen Greene Press).

15 Curt Bruce and Jill Grossman, *Revelations of New England Architecture* (New York: Grossman Publ., 1975).

16 Marion M. Ohman, A History of *Missouri's Counties, County Seats and Courthouse Squares* (University of Missouri Press, 1983).

17 J.B. Jackson, *Discovering the Vernacular Landscape* (New Haven: Yale University Press, ©1984).

18, 19, 20,21 *American Architect and Building News*, Sept. 15, 1909.

22 Richard Pare, ed., *Court House - A Photographic Document* (New York: Horizon Press, 1978).

23 Drawing by Matthew J. Bell and Linda Micale.

24 Willard Robinson, *Texas Public Buildings of the Nineteenth Century* (Austin: University of Texas Press, 1978).

25 Courtesy of the John Carter Brown Library at Brown University.

26 Richard Pare, ed., *Court House - A Photographic Document* (New York: Horizon Press, 1978).

27,28 Robert Stafford and Matthew J. Bell, University of Maryland, School of Architecture, 1 March 1994.

URBAN PARADOX: DISTINCTIVE UBIQUITY

SUSAN NIGRA SNYDER

Susan Snyder teaches at the University of Pennsylvania and practices with CoCA, Company for the Civic Arts in Philadelphia.

Material culture as a medium of personal and group expression is an integral and telling aspect of any social system. People acquire material possessions and experiences to define themselves and to express their identity to others. Mary Douglas in *The World of Goods* explains the idea of consumption in the social system by demonstrating that it is part of the same need that drives all human activities; the need for people to relate to each other.[1] Consumption in this context is not about greed or competitive display, but about the use of material possessions and experiences to communicate social meaning. In this sense, leisure is a form of consumption, an activity centered on the acquisition of experiences through culture, recreation and entertainment.

In postwar decades, advances in telecommunication and increased mobility have created a new urban realm in which consumption is the impulse of contemporary life. Increased personal wealth along with reduced working hours has enabled nearly everyone, not only the most affluent, to have the time and the means for leisure. Contemporary leisure activities are no longer limited to weekends or seasonal vacations, but now take place within the same spatial and temporal domain as other daily urban activities: work, shopping, community, and civic activities.

In the industrial era, a city's location was limited to places that met the criteria necessary for industrial production and distribution. Historically, the location of one's home usually followed the location of the workplace. One can now live anywhere and still participate in the production and consumption of urban life. Communication and transportation technologies allow institutions of commerce to organize large numbers of people across great distances into a truly global socio-economic system. Characteristic of this system are

Seed storage facility.

activities and physical forms that are neither geographically nor culturally specific. The traditional hierarchy of place for purposes of work and consumption has been leveled, making all places equally suitable for nearly all activities.

Modern systems of production and consumption have created a global matrix so ubiquitous and accessible that it allows individuals to select and physically order their locales—geographically situated settings for activities—according to personal choices. These choices concern geographic locations, home, community, daily patterns, and leisure activities and involve characteristics—physical context, cultural heritage, or social structure that are embedded in the locale and cannot be easily reproduced elsewhere. The locale embodies individual choice and site-specificity; the global matrix, commonality and uniformity.

Although these may seem contradictory, both are needed to achieve an equilibrium in contemporary urban life. Each condition balances the other: monotony by unique situations, passive routine by intellectual and physical activity, placelessness by site-specificity. When leisure activities are site-specific, they further determine the characteristics of home, daily patterns and social life that produce a distinctive life-style. Together, the global matrix and the leisure-focused locale are recasting existing urban fabric and creating new settlements in rural landscapes that are instrumental in the development of contemporary urban form, from its geographic and spatial organization to its material culture, including architecture and the landscape.

One clear example that these changes have started to take hold is in the emergence of the "lone eagle", a professional who can locate anywhere because work can be accomplished with a computer, modem, fax machine, and an occasional trip to the airport. Lone eagles, or "modem cowboys" as they are known in the Rockies, typically choose to live in an isolated setting chosen for the quality of available everyday leisure activities as well as its scenic delight. Though they are physically remote from the marketplace, modern distribution makes most manufactured prod-

ucts available anywhere. If the lone eagle enjoys physical isolation, it is no longer at the expense of the limited scope of a small-town life.

Since 1991, economic growth in the mountain states has exceeded 5%, compared to 1% for the rest of the country. Unemployment there is lower, housing permit application higher, and in 1992 the region's population growth surpassed all other regions of the country. A large amount of the growth has occurred in Denver, the largest city in the region. Historically, the city's isolated location did not make it a major player in the nationally based industrial economy. Now, however, economic development agencies, low cost structure, a new airport, and advances in information technology contribute to the advantages of Denver's location. Moreover, Denver's location on a mile high plain at the edge of the Front Range of the Colorado Rockies offers a relatively mild climate with more than average daily sunshine, warm daily temperatures in winter, and spectacular mountain views. Access to the mountains is easy. Within one to two hours of the city, recreational resorts and national parks abound. Easy access to recreational activities contributes to the dominant life-style, culture and overall quality of life.

People choose to move to Denver because it is a location where a leisure-focused life-style is congruent with the amenities of physical geography and participation in the commerce of the global economy. Unencumbered by the order of an industrial economy, Denver offers new opportunities for a contemporary urban life not possible through re-inhabitation of older physical forms. Here, the imprint of a low density spatial order, necessary for agrarian production, can be easily overlaid with the new settlement patterns of the contemporary economy. The following collection of photographs documents sites that manifest the paradox inherent in the form of the contemporary city. They reveal the simultaneous experience of commonality and placelessness characteristic of global urban form with the experience of a distinctive local culture and cultivated life-style centered on site-specific leisure activities.

...he'd been a cowboy, a rustler, one of the best in the Sprawl...jacked into a custom cyberspace deck that projected his disembodied consciousness into the consensual hallucination that was the matrix. [2]

2, 3. Today, most people in the United States work in an office-based setting such as the Denver Tech Center. The product of this work, information, is easily transportable at a cost not affected by distance or location. Work is not tied to any specific geographic landscape or architectural form but requires only proximity to a regional airport, connection to a communication network, and flexible office space. Moreover, office parks, along with housing, shopping malls, airports and expressways, can now be built virtually anywhere. Urban form has become ubiquitous. That is, it occurs anywhere and everywhere at the same time, providing physical evidence of the emergence of a global society driven by the institutions of commerce.

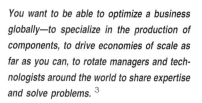

You want to be able to optimize a business globally—to specialize in the production of components, to drive economies of scale as far as you can, to rotate managers and technologists around the world to share expertise and solve problems. [3]

4, 5. A uniform landscape of consumer products and entertainment, made possible by the global structure of production, distribution and electronic media, extends virtually everywhere. Within this landscape, no one place has an advantage over another for access to the array of consumer opportunities. Five hundred channel interactive television promises to make an even wider choice of specialized goods and events available, further increasing homogeneity.

They're America's latest pioneers, those urban exiles who've gone back to the land following the migration of high-tech companies. In God's Country, they've created rural boomtowns with the highest socioeconomic levels outside the nation's major metropolitan areas. [4]

6, 7. Although just minutes west of I-470, Ken-Caryl Ranch is located in a valley of the foothills of the Front Range where temperatures are 10 degrees cooler, air cleaner and views extraordinary. Shared community amenities, the focus of this development, include a twenty mile path system, recreation facilities, an equestrian center, a community center and more than 60,000 acres of natural open space. The ubiquity of the typical housing development has been transformed into a unique planned community that creates a lifestyle focused on extensive daily leisure within the natural wilderness of the existing landscape.

One of the fundamental problems of prosperity is to sanction and to justify its enjoyment, to convince people that making their life enjoyable is moral, and not immoral. [5]

8, 9. Similar to urban nodes containing regional shopping malls or cultural districts, resorts, national parks and numerous other recreation destinations are also nodes within the multi-centered Denver area. Like the town square and Main Street of older urban forms, these leisure areas are places of social centrality. A wide range of people from different backgrounds and ages are brought together around common interests and activities.

...those who seek to invest in new service, information and high-tech industries may be swayed by the ambiance and cultural capital of cities and may have helped to speed up the reconversion strategies....[6]

10, 11. Downtown Fort Collins dates back 115 years to the early pioneering days of Colorado. The town's rich cultural history is evident in the architecture. This history has been combined with a mix of contemporary leisure activities—unique shopping, micro-brewing, recreation and cultural events—to create a place, unique within the homogenous contemporary landscape. By contrast, the myth of the Western frontier is accessible through the symbolic capital of consumer goods that can be purchased world-wide and used as personal markers of distant landscapes and lifestyles.

In conditions of modernity, place becomes increasingly phantasmagoric: that is to say, locales are thoroughly penetrated by and shaped in terms of social influences quite distant from them. What structures the locale is not simply that which is present on the scene; the "visible form" of the locale conceals the distanced relations which determine its nature. [7]

12, 13. Aspen combines the qualities and activities found in separate nodes of the Denver urban fabric: outdoor recreation, unique and generic shopping, cultural events, entertainment, spectacular alpine scenery and an historical setting, and even aspects of world class cities within the setting of a small village. The contrast of intimate scale and of events typical of major metropolitan centers creates an experience so unique and powerful that it attracts a global community.

NOTES

1 Mary Douglas and Brian Isherwood, *The World of Goods* (New York: W. W. Norton & Co., 1982).

2 William Gibson, *Neuromancer* (New York: Ace Books, 1984), 5.

3 William Taylor, "The Logic of Global Business", *Harvard Business Review* (March-April, 1991), 91-105.

4 Michael J. Weiss, *The Clustering of America* (New York: Harper and Row, 1988), 294.

5 Mark Poster, ed., *Jean Baudrillard: Selected Writings* (Stanford University Press, 1988).

6 Mike Featherstone, *Consumer Culture & Postmodernism* (London: Sage, 1991), 107.

7 Anthony Giddens, *The Consequences of Modernity* (Stanford: Stanford University Press, 1990), 18-19.

CREDITS

All photographs courtesy of the author.

Material for this article was made possible by a grant received by Ms. Snyder from the Research Foundation of the University of Pennsylvania. Scott H. Siekert assisted in research and preparation of this article.

WEST BANK INDUSTRIAL WORKERS' CLUB

BRIAN ANDREWS

Brian Andrews is Assistant Professor
of Architecture at the University of
Virginia.

At opposite ends of the architectural-political spectrum exist the idea of the pastoral and the idea of the civil. Any neo-Civil Architecture in America must reconcile these two opposing concepts while retaining the positive aspects of each. Unfortunately, many attempts to achieve a balance have resulted in suburban sprawl. There are, however, other spatial typologies that successfully occupy the architectural middle ground. The academic campus is one example which allows and encourages an active discourse between freedom and authority. Another example is the industrial building, exemplified in the factories of Ledoux, Behrens, Gropius and Albert Kahn. The Industrial Workers' Club, designed as an industrial civil project, attempts to reconcile the opposing concepts of pastoral and civil-of freedom and authority.

The project is located on the Mississippi River at Nine Mile Point, near the town of Bridge City, Louisiana, a satellite of New Orleans. A levee protects Bridge City from the river and creates the particular landscape of the site known as the "bature." The bature—frequently flooded and consisting primarily of mud, reeds, and water—is often considered a wasteland—perilous and unstable. Currently, the area near the levee is populated primarily with low income and unemployed industrial workers. Scattered among the small wooden shotgun shacks and low, brick ranch houses are four substantial generators which supply electricity to the City of New Orleans, archaeological remains of the giants of industry, colossal grain elevators along the levee, and abandoned monumental oil tanks. Decrepit monsters of dead industries litter the zone, transforming it into a sublime netherworld. Children play among the rusted hulls, using old storage tanks as a backdrop to their imaginations. It was this unique landscape, a testament to Louisiana's failed oil industry and lack of economic diversity, that served as an inspiration and catalyst for the project. The rich language of the landscape and the political need for economic diversity combined within the project to form a pluralistic architecture, on one level reflecting the existing social conditions and on another serving as a model for the future.

Continental Grain Elevator.

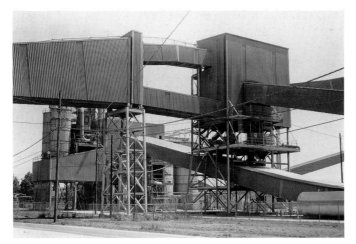

Continental Grain Conveyors.

View of Site at Rivers' Edge.

Site Plan of Five Mile Point.

The program for the Club includes recreational spaces: a gymnasium and sports fields, an educational retraining center, a theatre, a restaurant, a motel and an administration center. The diverse functions were broken down into a melange of parts: typological, material, structural, and symbolic. Forms and politics of the surrounding landscape—the causeway, ship, bridge, oil tank, wharf, bunker, grain conveyer and sheds—were treated as fragments and then re-assembled. This assemblage design approach allowed a great deal of liberty for personal interpretation; it is an approach which recognizes the active interchange between freedom and authority.

All of the elements of the program were constrained and knitted by the omnipresent, 520 foot long, exterior steel corridor or spine-like structure which is ramped and elevated. The spine's removal from the unstable ground plane implies a certain liberty from the natural and man-made forces of the site. Conversely, the spine, acting as a large exterior hallway, portrays the quintessence of control. The linear spine becomes the essence of the complex, acting as the primary vessel on two levels; initially it carries the occupants from one element to another, and then acts as a

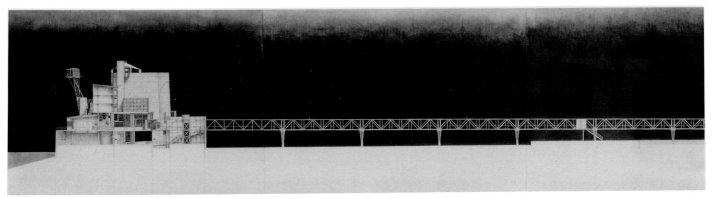

Site Section through Building at Entrance Causeway.

Site Model.

West Bank Industrial Workers' Club

Entrance View.

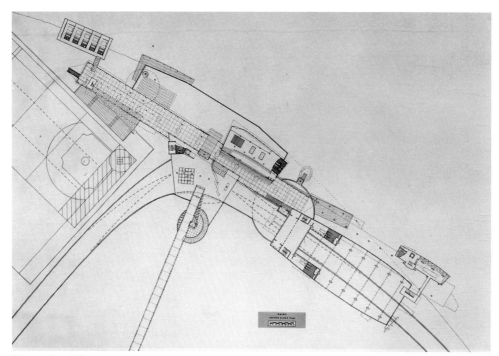

Entrance Level Plan.

Entrance Elevation.

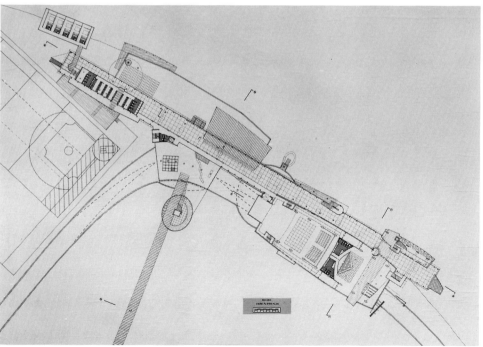

Third Level Plan.

View from River.

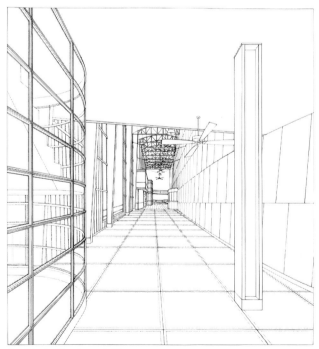

Corridor looking towards Theatre.

container and center of the club. This reversal, where the center has been transformed into an ephemeral linear sequence, is critical to the project's relationship to a more typological civil architecture. Historically, civil edifices such as courtrooms and meeting halls utilize an honorific approach to the building's center. In this club, however, the hallway—the most banal of typologies—has been re-interpreted to form the essential linear center.

This central spine of the project defies definition and identification according to standard rules. It is important to point out, however, that this is not a loss of center, but rather a mutation of center. Serving as a linear center, it organizes the sub-elements into a coherent sequence. Epicenters, or pavilions, manifest this interrelationship in their dispersed locations along the steel corridor. The design of these constituents reflects not only the landscape, but also the desired requisite industrial diversity of the state's economy in architectural terms. The development and identification of the "pavilions" evolved from an investigation of both the immediate political and site conditions, and the models of worker's clubs of the past, more specifically,

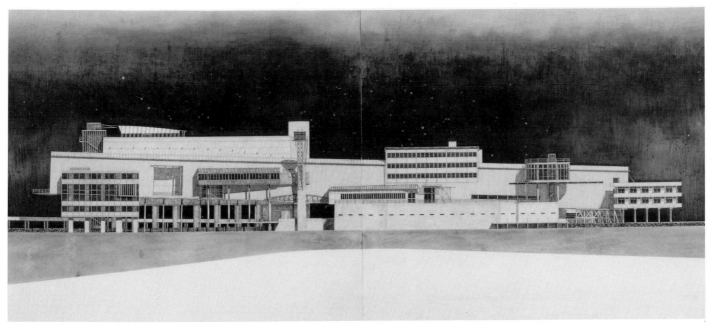

River Elevation.

the Soviet clubs of the 1920s. Not unlike those organizations, this club was intended to act as a "social condenser," a proposed hot-bed of political, social, industrial, physical, intellectual, educational, economic and cultural debate. Thus the edifice began to occupy a middle ground, not only between the pastoral and the civil, but also between capitalism and Marxist materialism.

The West Bank Industrial Workers' Club defies typical explanation: it has no front or back, its hierarchy seems to shift depending on its use. The surrounding landscape has infected, and affected, the various elements of the structure, resulting in a hybrid that is both representative and critical. The political landscape in which the building operates has challenged the Civil. The building both defers to and challenges the Civil resulting in a statement about politics and society that, while disquieting, is not discouraging.

PROJECT CREDITS

All figures courtesy of the author.
Project Team included: Beau Clowney, Peter Cornell, Paul Hanley, James Orsi, Gill Rampy, Rene Tan, Kristin Terry, Tobin Weaver, James Wilson.

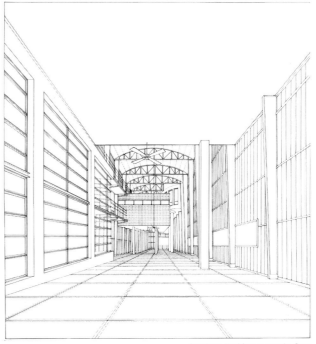

Corridor looking towards Gym.

BIOGRAPHICAL NOTES

BRIAN ANDREWS teaches design and architectural delineation as an Assistant Professor at the University of Virginia. He holds a Bachelor of Architecture degree from Tulane University, and a Master of Architecture from Princeton University. Mr. Andrews has worked in the offices of Ralph Lerner, Architect; Machado and Silvetti Architects; Schwartz/Silver Architects; and Koetter, Kim, & Associates. His work has appeared in the journals *Progressive Architecture*, *Architecture*, and *Crit 16*; and in the books *Machado/Silvetti: A Monograph, Architecture and Urbanism*, and *18 Houses*. Mr. Andrews has received several awards and citations for his work, and has been honored by the American Society of Architectural Perspectivists, the Architectural League of New York, the Boston Society of Architects, and the Association of Collegiate Schools of Architecture.

MATHEW J. BELL is an architect and an Assistant Professor at the University of Maryland School of Architecture. He earned his Bachelor of Architecture degree from the University of Notre Dame and his Master of Architecture in Urban Design from Cornell University. Mr. Bell has held teaching and administrative appointments at the University of Maryland, Cornell University and the University of Miami. He has been published in the *Cornell Journal of Architecture* and *The New City*; and lectures extensively on American urbanism. Mr. Bell has participated as a designer on Haymount, a traditional town in Caroline County,

Virginia and is the Co-Director of the Northeast Regional meeting of the Mayor's Institute for City Design. Mr. Bell has shared honors with Brian P. Kelly and Cheryl A. O'Neill for their entry in the international competition for the design of the Warsaw, Poland city center area. He also serves on the board of directors of the Neighborhood Design Center of Baltimore and Prince Georges County, Maryland and coordinates the ongoing ACSA documentation of American urban paradigms.

THEODORE L. BROWN is an Associate Professor at Syracuse University and a member of the Congress for New Urbanism. He received his Bachelor of Science in Architecture from the University of Virginia, a Master of Architecture from Princeton University, and is a Fellow of the American Academy in Rome. Mr. Brown is a co-partner in the firm Munly/Brown Architects, whose work has been shown in the United States and Italy.

MICHAEL DENNIS is a Professor of Architecture at the Massachusetts Institute of Technology and is Principal of Michael Dennis & Associates, based in Boston. His work in architectural and urban design and research has been recognized with several awards and citations by, among others, *Progressive Architecture*, the Architectural Institute of America, and the Graham Foundation for the Advanced Studies in the Fine Arts. A frequent lecturer, Mr. Dennis has also held Visiting Professorships at Yale

University, the University of Virginia, Rice University and Harvard University. Michael Dennis is author of the book *Court and Garden: From the French Hotel to the City of Modern Architecture*.

CHRISTOPHER FAUST holds a B.A. in Biology from St. Cloud State University and a M.S. in Educational Media from the University of Wisconsin—LaCrosse. While at the University of Wisconsin he held a staff position at the National Fisheries Research Lab under the U.S. Fish and Wildlife Service where he received a Special Achievement Award in 1979. Since 1987 he has continued explorations into the visual arts and in 1989 he received the McKnight Artist Fellowship in photography. He has pursued such photographic themes as wilderness ecology, the loss of Midwestern grain elevators and Lake Superior ore boats. In 1992 he received a second McKnight Fellowship for his work with the Suburban Documentation Project.

DONALD B. GENASCI is Principal of the firm Donald B. Genasci and Associates. He received his Bachelor of Architecture degree from the University of Oregon, a Certificate of Urban Design from the Architectural Association in London, and a Master of Arts in Architectural History and Theory from Essex University. Mr. Genasci worked for the London Borough of Southwark before opening his first office, Genasci and Liventson Architects. He has taught at the Architectural Association, the Polytechnic of Central London, Princeton University, Harvard University, and the University of Oregon where he has been a Professor since 1986. Mr. Genasci's work has merited numerous honors, including a Progressive Architecture Award for the Eugene Riverfront Development; and citations for the West Hollywood Civic Center Competition, and the Native American Preparatory School.

BRIAN KELLY is Associate Professor of Architecture at the University of Maryland at College Park. He received his Bach-

elor of Architecture from the University of Notre Dame and his Master of Architecture in Urban Design from Cornell University. He has taught at Syracuse University, Arizona State University, the University of Miami in Coral Gables, and Catholic University of America. He has practiced architecture with Skidmore Owings and Merril in Chicago, and with Peterson Littenburg Architects and Barnett Peterson, both in New York. He currently practices as an urban design and campus planning consultant. Mr. Kelly has written extensively on the role of tradition in the context of modernity; and has appeared in such publications as *Reflections 8*, *Planning*, *Urban Design Visions and Reflections: Collected Essays*, and *Contemporary Masterworks*.

ANNE MUNLY received her Bachelor of Science in Architecture from the University of Virginia and a Master of Architecture from Princeton University. She has taught and practiced architecture in both Italy and the United States and currently teaches architectural design and American urbanism at Syracuse University where she is an Assistant Professor. As a partner in Munly/Brown Architects, she has engaged in many competitions, including the Casa Piu Bella and Washington Ridge competitions. Ms. Munly has received research grants from the NEA and the Boston Foundation for Architecture in support of her work in American urbanism.

FRANK EDGERTON MARTIN holds a B.A. in Philosophy from Vassar College and an M.S. in Landscape Architecture from the University of Wisconsin—Madison where he studied landscape history and preservation. His background includes scientific as well as historical approaches to landscape research. He has published writings on landscape history and theory in such journals as *Design Book Review*, *Design Quarterly*, *Landscape Journal*, and *Landscape Architecture*. Mr. Martin is employed as a writer and research coordinator for Hammel Green and Abrahamson architects in Minneapolis where he specializes in master planning and historic garden design. In 1993, he received a Critic's Travel Grant from the Center for Arts Criticism for his work with the Suburban Documentation Project.

OMID MIRARABSHAHI is an Associate in the firm Donald B. Genasci and Associates where he specializes in urban design and planning. Recently, his work has focussed on neighborhood development projects involving community action groups. He received his Bachelor of Architecture degree from the University of Oregon in 1988. Mr. Mirarabshahi finds additional artistic expression outside of architecture through painting, which is currently being exhibited at local venues in Portland.

NEAL I. PAYTON is an Associate professor of Architecture at The Catholic University of America and a practicing architect and town planner in Washington, D.C. He holds professional degrees in architecture from Carnegie Mellon University and Syracuse University, and has taught at the University of Virginia, Rice University, and Washington University in St. Louis. He is currently working on a book on the Patrick Geddes plan for Tel Aviv for which he has recently received a Graham Foundation grant.

JONATHAN ROSE is President of the Affordable Housing Construction Corporation, a real estate development and consulting firm based in Katonah, New York. Mr. Rose holds a Bachelor of Arts in Psychology and Philosophy from Yale University, and a Master of Regional Planning from the University of Pennsylvania, where he currently serves on the school's Board of Governors. Mr. Rose is extensively involved in a variety of land use and planning organizations, acting as Trustee for the Project for Public Space, the Land Trust Alliance, and the Regional Plan Association. He is a member of the North Salem Town Affordable Housing Committee, and served as a former Trustee of the Westchester Land Trust. Mr. Rose is an active member of the Urban Land Institute, the American Planning Association, and the Social Venture Network. A frequent lecturer, Mr. Rose has spoken to the Aspen Design Conference, Yale Law School, and the First Congress for the New Urbanism. Additionally, Jonathan Rose was the founder of Gramavision Records, a producer of jazz and contemporary classical recordings.

MARK SCHIMMENTI is principal of Mark M. Schimmenti, Architect and Urbanist, and Associate Professor of Architecture in City and Town Design at the University of Virginia. Following an honorable discharge from the United States Navy in 1976, Mr. Schimmenti studied at the University of Florida where he earned his Bachelor of Design in Architecture in 1978, and a Master of Architecture in History Theory and Criticism in 1980. He worked with the firms Venturi, Rauch & Scott Brown and Duany Platter-Zyberk, before opening his own firm in 1989. Mr. Schimmenti's professional recognition includes a Progressive Architecture Citation in Urban Design, and an Award for Excellence from the Virginia Chapter of the American Planning Association. He is an itinerant lecturer and critic and a member of the Congress for New Urbanism.

SUSAN NIGRA SNYDER received her Bachelor of Arts from Mount Holyoke College and a Master of Architecture from the University of Pennsylvania. She is a registered architect in the Commonwealth of Pennsylvania and practices with the Company for the Civic Arts (CoCA). Ms. Snyder serves as the Chair of the Advisory Board of Design for the Redevelopment Authority of Philadelphia and is also a member of that organization's Fine Arts Committee. Since 1983, Ms. Snyder has been a member of the faculty of the Department of Architecture at the University of Pennsylvania.

PETER DAVID WALDMAN was born in New York City in 1943. After receiving his B.A. and M.A. degrees in Architecture from Princeton University, he spent two years in Arequipa, Peru, as Chief Architect for the Junta de la Rehabilitacion y Dessarrolo De Arequipa in conjunction with the United States Peace Corps. Mr.

Waldman has since taught at Rice University, the University of Cincinnati, and Princeton; and has held visiting professorships at the University of Texas, Harvard Graduate School of Design, and Southern California Institute of Architecture. Since 1992, he has taught design and theory at the University of Virginia. Mr. Waldman has lectured and exhibited his work across the United States, and his work has been featured in such journals as *Global Architecture*, *American Craft*, *The Princeton Journal*, *Progressive Architecture*, *Center*, *Texas Architect*, and *Modulus 22: Craft and Architecture*. Mr. Waldman is currently building his own home in Charlottesville, Virginia.

CARROLL WILLIAM WESTFALL was born in Fresno, California. He received his B.A. in the History of Art from the University of California in 1961, an M.A. from the University of Manchester, England in 1963, and his Ph.D. from Colombia University in 1967. After teaching at Amherst College, Mr. Westfall joined the faculty of the University of Illinois at Chicago, and in 1982 moved to the University of Virginia, where he served as the Chair of the Department of Architectural History in the School of Architecture. Mr. Westfall has lectured and written broadly on Medieval, Renaissance, Napoleonic, and Jeffersonian architecture and art. His books include *In This Most Perfect Paradise* and *Architectural Principals in the Age of Historicism*, which was co-authored with Robert Jan van Pelt.

Modulus 23 *thanks the following people for their generous contributions:*

BENEFACTORS

Robert D. Dripps, 3rd

William McDonough + Partners

New York Review of Books

Lucia Phinney

Robert A.M. Stern Architects

UVA School of Architecture Design Council

UVA Student Council Appropriations Committee

UVA Deans Forum

Mario di Valmarana

PATRONS

Smith Miller + Hawkinson, Architects

Kenneth Youngblood

DONORS

Charles F. Johnson

Judith Kinnard

Charles T. Matheson

Elizabeth Meyer

James Nagle

Olson/Sundberg Architects, Inc.

Kenneth Schwartz

COLOPHON

Modulus 23 was designed by the editorial staff of Modulus in Charlottesville, Virginia. The text was electronically composed on an Apple® Macintosh™ SE using Aldus Pagemaker®, version 4.0. It was processed on a Linotronic™ 530 printer at 2540 dpi and reproduced through offset lithography on 80# Sterling Satin by BookCrafters of Fredericksburg, Virginia. Text design employs Times, Avant Garde, and Helvetica typefaces.